Old Testament—Series A

by Edward C. Grube

SAINT LOUIS

Copyright © 1995 Concordia Publishing House
3558 S. Jefferson Avenue, St. Louis, MO 63118-3968
Manufactured in the United States of America

Library of Congress Cataloging-in-Publication Data.

Grube, Edward C., 1947–
   Object Lessons: Old Testament, series A / by Edward C. Grube.
   ISBN 0-570-04822-2 (Series A)

   Includes indexes.
   Contents: [1] Series A — [2] Series B — [3] Series C
   1. Children's sermons. 2. Church year sermons. 3. Object teaching. I. Title.

BV 4315.G78   1993
252'.53   92-42405

1 2 3 4 5 6 7 8 9 10   04 03 02 01 00 99 98 97 96 95

To Allison and Aaron—
two of Jesus' lights shining in my life

Contents

*Introduction*_____

God proclaimed His Good News in the Old Testament. We find it in passages from the Pentateuch, prophets, Proverbs, poets, and protagonists. Yes, God always has Good News. And the Good News sounds even better against the backdrop of the Law. That's what makes object lessons from the Old Testament a delight to create and present.

Enjoy yourself as you prepare and present the messages. A light heart and an enthusiastic voice will do much to capture your active audience's attention. Messages are geared for children five through eight years old, but speak loud enough for the whole congregation to hear—they appreciate object lessons in faith, too. Photocopy and enlarge the pages so they're easy to read, or use the lessons to create *better* lessons from your own experiences as God's child. However you employ this book, practice out loud. Hear how the words flow or twist. Experiment with different inflections, gestures, and facial expressions.

Most objects suggested in this book are found in your desk, kitchen, garage, toy box, church office, or sanctuary. Practice handling the objects while you speak so you don't end up a juggling act! Consider recruiting adolescent or teenage helpers for the most challenging lessons. (Two lessons require a simple, homemade puppet.)

Object lessons are appropriate in several different settings. If the children's message occurs during worship services, these object lessons will be more effective when delivered shortly after the Bible readings. Each object lesson relates and refers to the Old Testament lesson for the day. If your congregation does not follow the A-B-C Lutheran lectionary, you will need to adapt certain parts of the message. You may also find these object lessons suitable for use in Sunday school, weekday school, or school chapel services.

Finally, include the Holy Spirit in your plans and presentations. Pray for the Spirit's power to work through you and your message. And don't fret about your "effectiveness." St. Paul says, "I came to you in weakness and fear, and with much trembling.

My message and my preaching were not with wise and persuasive words, but with a demonstration of the Spirit's power, so that your faith might not rest on men's wisdom, but on God's power" (1 Cor. 2:3–5).

May God bless your ministry with children.

Fire Power

ADVENT 1: Is. 2:1–5; Rom. 13:11–14; Matt. 24:37–44 or Matt. 21:1–11

Text. He will judge between the nations and will settle disputes for many peoples. They will beat their swords into plowshares and their spears into pruning hooks. Nation will not take up sword against nation, nor will they train for war anymore. Come, O house of Jacob, let us walk in the light of the LORD. *Is. 2:4–5*

Teaching aids. A clear light bulb (optional); a candle and matches. (The first Advent candle might be lighted at this time.)

Gospel nugget. Jesus brings peace and mercy to His people.

Has anyone ever told you "Don't play with these?" (*Show the matches.*) Why not? (*Encourage responses.*)

Matches start fires, and fires are often dangerous. As you know, fire can destroy people, houses, trees, and animals.

Fire is sometimes used to describe people. If you had a fiery temper, how would you act? (*Invite responses.*) That's correct. You would easily get angry.

When we talk about hell, we usually think of fire. In fact, some people picture the devil as a fiery red monster with horns and a pointed tail.

Is fire good for anything? Fire has several good uses. For example, it keeps us warm. On chilly winter days, furnaces heat our homes. Most furnaces have little fires inside that create heat. The furnace sends heat through pipes to warm the house.

Fire is also good for giving light. Light bulbs have thin wires enclosed in glass. (*Show the light bulb.*) Electricity makes those thin wires glow with fire so we can see at night. Before people had light bulbs, they used candles for light. (*Show the candle.*) When lighted with a match (*strike a match*), the candle glows with warm light (*light the candle*).

We don't need candles to light our homes anymore, but we use them for decorations. For what events do we light candles? (*Encourage responses.*) Yes, we light candles to celebrate birthdays. We see candles in church, too.

Since today is the first day of Advent, it's a good time to light an Advent candle like this one (*indicate the Advent candle*). The lighted candle reminds us that Jesus is the Light of the world. He has fire power! But what does it mean to be the Light of the world? Let me explain.

Before the birth of Jesus, people felt like they lived in darkness. Oh, they believed God's promise to send a Savior, but they wanted to actually see Him and know Him. Their hopes came true when Jesus was born in Bethlehem. He was like a bright light that did away with darkness and brought joy to His people.

Jesus lights our lives, too. He is like a brilliant night light. Do you have a night light in your house? What does a night light do for you? (*Encourage responses.*) That's right. A night light makes us feel peaceful and safe. Jesus' light is that way, too. He gives us peace because we belong to Him.

God promised to send peace in the Old Testament reading for today. Listen. (*Read the text.*)

That's what Advent is about. *Advent* means "coming." Jesus will come again someday. And when He does, He will bring lasting peace. We'll get along with everyone. Best of all, we'll be safe and warm sitting next to the Light of the world.

Prayer. Dear Jesus, warm us with Your fire power. Give us fire power to tell others You are coming again. Amen.

*Unusual Gifts*_____

ADVENT 2: Is. 11:1–10; Rom. 15:4–13; Matt. 3:1–12

Text. The wolf will live with the lamb, the leopard will lie down with the goat, the calf and the lion and the yearling together; and a little child will lead them. The cow will feed with the bear, their young will lie down together, and the lion will eat straw like the ox. The infant will play near the hole of the cobra, and the young child put his hand into the viper's nest. They will neither harm nor destroy on all My holy mountain, for the earth will be full of the knowledge of the LORD as the waters cover the sea. In that day the Root of Jesse will stand as a banner for the peoples; the nations will rally to Him, and His place of rest will be glorious. *Is. 11:6–10*

Teaching aid. A box wrapped as a gift.

Gospel nugget. Jesus is the best and most unusual gift from God.

What do you look forward to at Christmas? (*Invite responses.*) Waiting for Christmas is so exciting. Gifts, family visits, and special foods! We look forward to Christmas all year.

I found this present wrapped and waiting for me. I wonder what is inside. Maybe it's something I need like (*mention some things you hope for*). Perhaps it's something I don't really need, but would really enjoy like (*mention several items from your wish list*). I hope it's not (*mention something distasteful*). The most unusual Christmas present I ever received was (*mention an unusual gift or one that you found impractical or useless*). Now that was truly an unusual gift!

What was the best Christmas gift you ever received? (*Invite *responses.*) The best Christmas gift ever was the one God gave to every person. Jesus was God's gift to all people who ever lived as well as to all those who aren't even born yet. And how much we need Him! All people sin, and Jesus came to forgive our sins. No wonder we're excited about celebrating His birth!

Did you know that Jesus will come back someday? He'll bring some unusual gifts when He returns. God told us about these unusual gifts in today's Bible reading. See if you can tell why these gifts are unusual. (*Read the text.*)

Wolves, leopards, and lions usually eat animals like lambs, goats, and calves. The Bible says that even snakes won't be dangerous. All this sounds like the Garden of Eden, where Adam and Eve led perfectly happy and safe lives.

Jesus will bring those amazing gifts when He comes again. Oh yes, He's coming again. Just as Jesus' birth surprised the shepherds, His next coming will surprise people, too. When Jesus comes again, we'll see Him decorated in bright clothing, surrounded by angels and beautiful music. Sound exciting? It is. That's why each year before Christmas, we celebrate Advent. Advent is a time of waiting—waiting for Christmas and Christmas gifts—waiting for Jesus to come again with even greater gifts.

What can we do while we wait? We can give gifts to others because God gave the greatest gift to us. We can tell others that if Christmas gets them excited, just wait until Jesus comes again. Let's pray for His next coming.

Prayer. Dear Jesus, we thank You for coming to save us from our sins. Come again, soon. We want to live with You forever. Amen.

Super HighWay_____

ADVENT 3: Is. 35:1–10; James 5:7–10; Matt. 11:2–11

Text. And a highway will be there; it will be called the Way of Holiness. The unclean will not journey on it; it will be for those who walk in that Way; wicked fools will not go about on it ... and the ransomed of the LORD will return. They will enter Zion with singing; everlasting joy will crown their heads. Gladness and joy will overtake them, and sorrow and sighing will flee away. *Is. 35:8, 10*

Teaching aid. Make a street or road sign out of cardboard or paper. Print *HighWay of Holiness* on it.

Gospel nugget. Jesus is the only Way to eternal life.

What are your travel plans this Christmas holiday? (*Encourage responses.*) How will you get there? (*Encourage responses.*)

We have many ways to travel. When you traveled up here, you used your feet. Back when Jesus was born, most people traveled on their feet. If they had many miles to travel, they rode animals like donkeys or camels.

Mary and Joseph walked along dusty roads on their trip to Bethlehem where Jesus was born. Many years later, Jesus Himself walked paths and dirt roads as He told people about God's love, forgave their sins, and invited them to follow Him. Jesus even told people which road led to heaven. He said, "Take the Way of Holiness." (*Show the street or road sign.*)

The Way of Holiness? It must be some kind of superhighway. I've heard of _____ Street and Interstate (or highway) _____, but I've never seen the highway Jesus talked about. Let's see what the Bible says about this highway. (*Read the text.*)

The Way of Holiness sounds like a really super highway. Did

you hear what kind of people travel on it? The Bible says it's not a road for wicked people. Only the righteous will travel on it. Are you righteous, or are you wicked? (*Invite responses.*)

Believe me, you are righteous. Righteous means that you are holy in God's sight, so the Way of Holiness (*point to the sign*) must be for you. Jesus made us holy when He died on the cross to take away our sins. We may travel on the Way of Holiness because we believe in Jesus. Truly wicked people don't believe in Him. They don't want His love or forgiveness. The Way of Holiness is not for them.

Did you hear where the Way of Holiness (*refer to the sign*) goes? The Bible calls the place Zion, but Zion is just another name for heaven—the place where God lives. It's also the place where you and I and all Christians will live.

If you're going away this Christmas, I'm sure you will prepare for the trip—even if it's a short one. Traveling along the Way of Holiness (*point to the sign*) requires some preparation, too. And do I have good news for you! You're preparing right now. You prepare to meet God when you listen to His Word. When you pray and when you ask forgiveness for the things you do wrong, you also get ready for your trip to heaven.

It's the Advent season. Advent is a time to think about meeting Jesus face to face—a time to prepare for our trip to heaven.

Prayer. Please pray with me. Thank You, Lord Jesus, for directing us to the Way of Holiness. Keep us on this road until we meet You in heaven. Amen.

What to Expect_____

ADVENT 4: Is. 7:10–14 (15–17); Rom. 1:1–7; Matt. 1:18–25

Text. Therefore the Lord Himself will give you a sign: The virgin will be with child and will give birth to a son, and will call Him Immanuel. *Is. 7:14*

Teaching aids. A knife, fork, and spoon; ribbon and/or wrapping paper; and Baby Jesus from a nativity set.

Gospel nugget. Jesus made us His own and prepares us for His arrival.

What do you expect when you see these? (*Reveal the eating utensils; invite responses.*) When we see knives, forks, and spoons, we expect to eat.

What do you expect when you come to church? (*Invite responses.*) Yes, we expect to pray, sing songs, hear stories from the Bible, and listen to the pastor.

Perhaps you've seen things like these lately. (*Show the ribbon and wrapping paper.*) What do you expect when you see ribbon and wrapping paper? (*Invite responses.*) Of course, Christmas presents come wrapped in ribbon and paper.

Here is something else you see this time of year. (*Show the figure of Baby Jesus.*) What is coming soon when you see this? (*Invite responses.*) Christmas is coming.

The (*indicate each*) knife, fork, spoon, ribbon, wrapping paper, and Baby Jesus are signs of things to come. Signs like these help us get ready for important events. God gave people many signs to help them get ready for things to come.

Before Jesus' birth, people wanted signs to help them remember God's promise of a Savior. Isaiah wrote about one of those

14

signs. You heard it in today's Old Testament Bible reading. Listen again. (*Read the text.*)

What did Jesus do after He was born? (*Encourage responses.*)

Jesus prepared people for heaven. As a young man, Jesus walked from village to village doing God's work. He wanted everyone to believe He was God's Son and that He came to forgive sinners. Jesus not only talked about God's love, but He showed it. He healed sick people and made blind people see. Jesus cured people who couldn't walk, and He even brought several people back to life after they died. All of Jesus' teaching and miracles were signs that He was God's true Son, the real-life Savior.

Then Jesus died. He loves us so much that He died to take away our sins. Jesus rose from the dead, too. That happened on Easter, and it was an amazing sign of things to come.

When Jesus rose from the dead, it was a sign of what will happen to us. With all these wonderful signs about our future, I think we should give other people some signs—signs that will help them believe what we believe—that Jesus is our Savior. What kind of signs can we give? (*Encourage responses.*)

One sign is especially good this time of year. We can say "Merry Christmas." Those words are a sign that you believe in Jesus. Another sign is a Christmas tree. Have you noticed how Christmas trees are pointed at the top? You might remind people that Christmas trees aim at heaven, and Jesus points the way to get there.

Prayer. Dear Lord Jesus, thank You for giving us faith to believe that You're our Savior. Let everything we do and everything we say be signs that show others Your love. Amen.

Muscles

THE NATIVITY: Is. 52:7–10; Heb. 1:1–9; John 1:1–14

Text. The LORD will lay bare His holy arm in the sight of all the nations, and all the ends of the earth will see the salvation of our God. *Is. 52:10*

Teaching aid. The arm of one or more participants.

Gospel nugget. God sent Jesus to destroy the power of sin.

Merry Christmas! I hope you all enjoy today's celebration. We'll talk more about Christmas in a few moments, but right now I need to ask a favor. Will you make a muscle? (*Demonstrate with your own arm. Feel the children's muscles.*) Wow! Those are fine muscles. You must be very strong.

Do you think babies have strong arm muscles? Not really. They have very strong cry muscles, but not very strong arm muscles. Do you think Baby Jesus had strong arm muscles? (*Encourage answers.*) Baby Jesus was a real baby, so His arms were tiny and thin. Jesus looked weak, but the prophet Isaiah said that Jesus was really strong. Listen. (*Read the text.*)

Jesus was strong enough to save all people. But save them from what?

God's people, the Jews, were unhappy. They didn't have a country of their own. Other countries had defeated them in wars, and they had become prisoners or slaves. When Jesus was born, the Romans were in charge, and the Jews wanted someone to save them.

The Jews remembered God's promise. He said, "Someday I will send a Savior who will rescue you." The Jews hoped for a strong king who could defeat the Romans and take charge of the

Jewish people. Do you think Baby Jesus looked much like a king? No, He looked like a baby.

When Jesus grew older, He didn't look like a strong king either. He had no crown, no throne, no expensive jewelry, no castle. But Jesus was a powerful king. He didn't show His power by bossing people around or making rules. King Jesus helped people. He walked into the poorest neighborhoods and told people that He loved them even though others treated them badly. Jesus loved people whom others found hard to love. He told the people marvelous news: "I forgive your sins. Now give up evil and follow Me. I'll save you."

Those who loved Jesus and followed Him were in for a shock. How they must have cried when their loving King died on the cross! But that was part of God's plan to save them. It was part of His plan to save us, too. And though King Jesus died on the cross, He also came back to life on Easter. King Jesus had the power to overcome sin, death, and Satan.

King Jesus makes us strong. He gives power to those who believe in Him. Out of thankfulness and joy, we use Jesus' power as He used it. We have Jesus' power to be kind and generous, not just at Christmas, but throughout the year. So drop off a can or two of food at the food pantry for those in need. Give clothing you outgrow to (*name local agency*). Use Jesus' power to forgive others when they make you angry or when they do bad things. And seek God's power for yourself through prayer, too. Why don't we exercise our prayer muscles right now? Please pray with me.

Prayer. Dear King Jesus, thank You for giving us Your power. Help us use it wisely. Bring hope to all whose Christmas isn't as happy as ours. Help us find ways to make their Christmas merry. We pray in Your name. Amen.

Thank-You Notes_____

CHRISTMAS 1: Is. 63:7–9; Gal. 4:4–7; Matt. 2:13–15, 19–23

Text. I will tell of the kindnesses of the LORD, the deeds for which He is to be praised, according to all the LORD has done for us—yes, the many good things He has done for the house of Israel, according to His compassion and many kindnesses. *Is. 63:7*

Teaching aid. A thank-you note or card (used or unused).

Gospel nugget. The Lord in His loving-kindness and grace chose to save each of us.

What did you get for Christmas? What gifts did you give? Why do people give gifts? (*Encourage responses.*)

Did you say thank you for each of your gifts? Maybe some of you even used one of these. (*Show the thank-you note.*) We appreciate people who love us, and we want them to know how we feel. That's why we say thank you or send thank-you notes.

When you said your prayers on Christmas, did you thank Jesus for coming to take away our sins? I guess we might easily forget in all the excitement, so let's thank Him right now—before we forget again. Repeat the words of the prayer after I say them. Ready?

Dear Jesus (*wait for the children to repeat phrases*), ... thank You for coming at Christmas. ... Thank You for taking away my sins. ... Keep my heart ... always thankful to You. ... Amen. ...

Let's talk about your Christmas gifts again. What will you do with them? (*Encourage responses.*) I'm sure you will play with your toys and games. If you got new clothing, you will probably wear it often. And do you expect people to use the gifts you gave? We know people appreciate our gifts when they actually use them.

It's the same with Jesus.

Jesus gave us the gift of forgiveness. That was a most important gift. What would happen if our sins weren't forgiven? (*Invite responses.*) That's right. We would not go to heaven. The devil would torture us instead. Forgiveness is important! How often should we ask Jesus to forgive us? (*Invite answers.*) We need to ask forgiveness each day because we sin each day. Let's ask Jesus to forgive us right now. Remember to say the words after me.

Dear Jesus, ... We hate sin, ... but we often do wrong anyway. ... We are sorry. ... Thank You ... for taking away our sins. ... Please help us ... do the right thing ... next time. ... Amen. ...

When you do something wrong against someone, you know you have Jesus' forgiveness, but it's good to ask the wronged person's forgiveness, too.

Forgiveness is a terrific gift to use often—not only for ourselves, but also for others. Can you think of anyone who needs your forgiveness? Sometimes people do things that aren't very nice. That's a good time to use the gift Jesus gave you. Tell them you forgive them. Forgiveness is the perfect gift to share.

Let's close with one more prayer. We'll use part of today's Old Testament Bible reading to praise God. Don't forget to repeat after me.

Prayer. I will tell ... of the kindnesses of the Lord, ... the deeds ... for which He is to be praised, ... according to all the Lord has done for us. ... Amen. ...

Cover Up_____

CHRISTMAS 2: Is. 61:10–62:3; Eph. 1:3–6, 15–18; John 1:1–18

Text. I delight greatly in the LORD; my soul rejoices in my God. For He has clothed me with garments of salvation and arrayed me in a robe of righteousness, as a bridegroom adorns his head like a priest, and as a bride adorns herself with her jewels. *Is. 61:10*

Teaching aids. Small scraps of paper and a clean cloth large enough to cover the scraps (*sprinkle the scraps of paper on the floor before the children assemble*); a wastebasket.

Gospel nugget. Jesus cleaned up our sins through His death and resurrection.

I wonder who left this mess. (*Indicate the scraps.*) Church is no place to be sloppy. Good thing I have this cloth. (*Place the cloth over the scraps.*) There! Now we can't see the litter.

I hate litter, don't you? It's hard to understand why anyone would leave a mess for others to clean. Yet, that's exactly what we do with our sins. We litter everything with our sins.

Whenever we do wrong, we make others unhappy. Often, we make ourselves unhappy, too. Worst of all, we make Jesus unhappy. Too bad we can't cover sins as easily as we cover other litter!

Lots of people try to cover up their own sins. Take Adam and Eve for example. What did they do after disobeying God? (*Invite answers.*) They tried to hide, and when God asked what they were doing, they made excuses. Then they tried to blame someone else for their wrongdoing. What a mistake! You can't fool God.

Have you ever done something wrong and tried to hide it? I think most people want to keep their wrongdoing a secret because they're embarrassed, afraid, or ashamed. But do I have good news! We don't need to cover up our sins.

God already knows we are sinners just as He knew about Adam and Eve. Our sins make God angry and sad. It doesn't help to cover up our sins.

Remember those scraps of paper? Well, (*lift the cover*) they're still here. The cloth only covered them for awhile. Instead of covering them, I should have cleaned them up.

A few weeks ago we celebrated Jesus' birth. That's when Jesus began to clean up our sins. About 30 years later, Jesus finished His job. Do you remember where He finished it? (*Invite responses.*) Yes, Jesus finished His work on the cross, where He died to clean up our sins. Jesus did what we can't do by ourselves.

As I said before, our sins are like this litter. We can't cover them. We don't have to. Jesus took them away completely. (*Clean up the litter and put it in the wastebasket.*) When God sees what kind of people we are, He doesn't see our sins. He sees holy and righteous believers in Jesus. How does that make you feel?

If you feel happy, then you'll understand the words from one of today's Bible readings. (*Read the text.*)

Let's end with prayer.

Prayer. Dear Jesus, thank You for dressing us in robes of righteousness. Thanks to You, we are clean and holy in God's sight. Help us tell others they need not cover up their own sins. Their Savior made them clean. In His name we pray. Amen.

Look over There!___

EPIPHANY: Is. 60:1–6; Eph. 3:2–12;
Matt. 2:1–12

Text. See, darkness covers the earth and thick darkness is over the peoples, but the LORD rises upon you and His glory appears over you. *Is. 60:2*

Teaching aids. A plastic bandage taped to your forehead; the Bible, baptismal font, communion ware and cross, especially in their normal setting in the chancel.

Gospel nugget. God still points the way to Jesus just as He did for the Wise Men.

Hello, everyone. What did you notice first about me this morning? It's hard to miss the bandage on my forehead. It draws attention to me, doesn't it? (*Remove the bandage.*) Today we will see what God uses to draw attention to Jesus.

We celebrate Epiphany today. Epiphany is when the Wise Men visited Jesus. God placed a special star in the sky when Jesus was born. And that star attracted the attention of several Wise Men. They knew something mighty important had happened, so they traveled many miles until they came to the spot beneath the star. And what did they find? (*Invite answers.*) That's right. They found Jesus, and they treated Him like the King He was. The Wise Men praised and honored Jesus with expensive gifts. And perhaps they remembered Isaiah's words. (*Read the text.*)

The star is gone, but God still points people to Jesus. How does He do that? (*Encourage responses.*) We have several of God's attention-getters right here in church.

Look over there. (*Point to the Bible.*) That book is the most important thing that points to Jesus. What book is that? Yes, it's the Bible. The Bible contains many true stories of how God promised to send a special King whose name would be Jesus. And the Bible provides many stories showing Jesus in action.

Let's find another thing that points to Jesus. Look over there. (*Point to the baptismal font.*) That baptismal font is like a marker that says, "Come to me. Here is where life with Jesus begins." And so, people from very old to very young are baptized. Faith comes alive in their hearts, and by one of God's mysterious miracles, they believe that Jesus is their Savior.

Now look over there. (*Point to the communion ware.*) Those pitchers and platters hold more than just bread and wine. They point to Jesus Himself because the bread and wine are also Jesus' body and blood. On the night before He died, Jesus celebrated the first Communion (or the Lord's Supper) with His disciples. Jesus told His disciples that the Lord's Supper brought forgiveness of sins and that eating it would help them remember Him.

There is at least one more thing in church that points to Jesus. Look over there. (*Point to the cross.*) The cross reminds us how Jesus died to take away our sins. It makes us think of how He suffered to save us. But notice, the cross is empty. Jesus didn't stay on the cross, nor did He remain dead. He rose on Easter and told us that we'll do the same thing after we die.

Where is Jesus now? Look over there. (*Point to a child's heart.*) Jesus lives with us and in us today. Now it's your turn to be a star like the one that pointed the Wise Men to Jesus. Show others that Jesus lives in you. Go in peace.

The Hero_____

THE BAPTISM OF OUR LORD: Is. 42:1–7; Acts 10:34–38; Matt. 3:13–17

Text. "Here is My servant, whom I uphold, My chosen one in whom I delight; I will put My Spirit on Him and He will bring justice to the nations. He will not shout or cry out, or raise His voice in the streets. A bruised reed He will not break, and a smoldering wick He will not snuff out. In faithfulness He will bring forth justice; He will not falter or be discouraged till He establishes justice on earth. In His law the islands will put their hope." This is what God the LORD says ... "I, the LORD, have called You in righteousness; I will take hold of Your hand. I will keep You and will make You to be a covenant for the people and a light for the Gentiles, to open eyes that are blind, to free captives from prison and to release from the dungeon those who sit in darkness. *Is. 42:1–7*

Teaching aid. A picture of a baby or a real baby (with cooperative parents!).

Gospel nugget. God dedicated His only Son to save and gather sinners into His kingdom.

Isn't this a charming baby? (*Show the picture or the child.*) Once you were this small. When your parents looked at you, they probably wondered what you would be like when you got older.

God had a child, too. His only Son was named Jesus. God didn't hope or dream about His Son. He knew exactly what Jesus would do. In fact, God told people about Jesus long before His Son was born. Listen to how God described His Son. (*Read the text.*)

Did you understand everything God said about Jesus? Perhaps I should explain. God meant that Jesus would care for all people, especially those who were treated poorly or unfairly. Jesus did just that. He went to the poor, sick, and suffering people with His good news and His healing.

When God talked about Jesus and bruised reeds and smoldering candles, He meant that Jesus would be kind and loving. We might think that Jesus would treat sinners like enemies, but Jesus did an amazing thing. Instead of destroying sinners, He forgave them and invited them to heaven.

God said that His Son wouldn't brag about the good things He did. He was right. Jesus cared only to heal people of their sins and other suffering.

God mentioned prisons and dungeons when He talked about His Son. Do you think Jesus helped criminals escape from jail? No, I think God was talking about people arrested for no good reason. But in a way, God was talking about us.

The devil wants to throw us in his jail. If he made us prisoners, we would have to do whatever he wanted. But Jesus won't let the devil make prisoners of us. He died to take away our sins and free us of the devil's power. God's Son is our very own hero!

God said more about His Son when Jesus was baptized. Jesus was baptized as a grown man—He was probably about 30 years old. God said, "Jesus is My Son and I'm very pleased with Him."

God says the same words about us, too. Jesus made us His brothers and sisters through Baptism. That makes us God's children. Let's thank Jesus for blessing us.

Prayer. Dear Jesus, thank You for giving us faith through Baptism. Help us imitate all the good things You have done for people. Amen.

Stir Up a Crowd_____

EPIPHANY 2: Is. 49:1–6; 1 Cor. 1:1–9; John 1:29–41

Text. He says: "It is too small a thing for You to be My servant to restore the tribes of Jacob and bring back those of Israel I have kept. I will also make You a light for the Gentiles, that You may bring My salvation to the ends of the earth." *Is. 49:6*

Teaching aids. A teaspoon, a tablespoon, and a large mixing spoon.

Gospel nugget. God made all people His own and sent Jesus to save them.

Today we'll see how much you know about spoons. Here comes spoon question number one. Which spoon would you use to feed a young child? (*Invite responses.*) That's correct. The teaspoon (*hold up the teaspoon*) would be ideal.

Now for spoon question number two. Which spoon would an adult use to serve mashed potatoes? Yes, indeed. The tablespoon (*indicate the tablespoon*) is excellent for serving food.

Here is spoon question number three. Which spoon would easily move mashed potatoes from a large pot to serving bowls? Of course. The large spoon is perfect for large jobs. (*Show the large mixing spoon.*)

These different-size spoons for different-size jobs remind me of today's Bible reading from Isaiah. Listen to a verse where God is talking to Jesus. (*Read the text.*)

Jesus had quite a job. God wanted Him to take the message of love "to the ends of the earth."

Let's try another quiz. This one is about reaching all people with God's good news. Let's pretend this teaspoon is just one person, the tablespoon is 25 pastors, and the large spoon is Jesus. Can you remember that? Good. Now for the first question. How could we reach one person with the good news that they're saved? (*Encourage responses. Review choices if necessary.*) Surely, one person can do that job. Is there anyone in your family or neighborhood that doesn't know about Jesus and His love for them? What can you do about it? (*Encourage responses.*)

Okay. Time for the next question. Pretend that no one in our whole state of (*name your state*) knows about Jesus. Which spoon, I mean which of our choices, would best reach all the people in (*state*)? Yes, the tablespoon stood for 25 pastors. It would take at least that many to reach all the people in our state. And it would take them quite a while to do the job. We certainly would do better if we had 50 or 100 or 1000 pastors for that job. If you remember, Jesus chose 12 men to help Him preach and teach. That number grew larger and larger, but Jesus always welcomes more preachers and teachers. Maybe someday you'll become a pastor, teacher, director of Christian education, church musician, or other church worker. That would be wonderful!

Are you ready for my last question? Who can help us tell the whole world that Jesus died for their sins? Of course, it's Jesus Himself. (*Indicate the largest spoon.*) In fact, we need Jesus even when we're telling only one person! He stirs us up (*make a stirring motion*) with His Holy Spirit so we can tell others about His love. Let's ask Him to stir us up right now.

Prayer. Dear Jesus, stir up our hearts and minds so that we can take Your message to our family, neighbors, and even the whole world. Amen.

From Dark to Light___

EPIPHANY 3: Is. 9:1–4; 1 Cor. 1:10–17; Matt. 4:12–23

Text. The people walking in darkness have seen a great light; on those living in the land of the shadow of death a light has dawned. *Is. 9:2*

Teaching aids. A variety of colored construction paper, including black, brown, gray, and other dark colors. Alternative: Plain white paper and a variety of colored crayons or markers.

Gospel nugget. Jesus brightens our dark, sinful lives with the good news of forgiveness and salvation.

Have you ever taken a color test? This morning we'll see how well you can tell bright colors from dark colors. Answer "dark" if the color I show is dark, and "bright" if the color I show is bright. Ready?

(*Substitute the colors of your choice.*) Is this red dark or bright? (*Bright.*) Is this grey dark or bright? (*Dark.*) How about this green? (*Dark.*) Yellow? (*Bright.*) (*Continue with several additional colors, and leave them on display.*)

Looking at all the colors before you, which one reminds you of night? (*Invite responses.*) Of course, dark blue is the color of night. Which color reminds you of the sun? Yes, this bright yellow is sunny colored.

Who will volunteer to divide these colors into two groups? (*Select volunteers.*) Make one pile of gloomy colors and another pile of cheerful colors. (*Allow time to complete the task.*) Thank you for helping. It looks like dark colors are on the gloomy pile and bright colors are on the cheerful pile. I think most of us agree with their choices.

God often talked about our life as if it were dark colored or bright colored. You heard one of those passages in today's Old Testament reading. Listen again. (*Read the text.*)

God said that people walked out of darkness into the light. Sin is like darkness. It's hard to see in the dark, so you don't know what or who is near you. How frightening! Sin, like the dark colors in this pile, makes us feel gloomy.

Pretend you're outside playing with some friends. Your mother calls you home. You go home—an hour after she calls. How will you feel when you face Mom? (*Invite responses; gloomy, frightened, sad.*) You would feel that way because you sinned by not obeying your mother right away. How would you feel when she said, "I'm disappointed that you disobeyed me, but I forgive you?" Of course, you would feel much better. It would be like walking from the darkness into the light. (*Demonstrate with the colored paper.*)

Let's think about another situation. You are standing in front of God. On one side of you is Jesus, and on the other side stands the devil. The devil points his finger at you—the way fingers point (*demonstrate*) when blaming you for something. The devil is talking to God. He says, "You know, God, this one is a sinner deluxe. Would you like to see the list of things he did wrong?" But Jesus' finger is moving, too. He motions you to come to Him (*demonstrate*). As you go to Jesus, He says, "You know, God, this one is a forgiven sinner. I died to take away his sins. They're all gone." Now that's walking from darkness into the light! (*Demonstrate.*) Wow, what a relief!

That's exactly how it is with Jesus. He takes us from the darkness of sin into the light of His love. Ask Him to keep His light in your hearts.

Show and Tell_____

EPIPHANY 4: Micah 6:1–8; 1 Cor. 1:26–31; Matt. 5:1–12

Text. He has showed you, O man, what is good. And what does the LORD require of you? To act justly and to love mercy and to walk humbly with your God. *Micah 6:8*

Teaching aid. The owners manual from your car.

Gospel nugget. God does not leave us guessing about what pleases Him; He tells us what He expects and empowers us to live godly lives.

Sometimes it's fun to guess, but guessing can cause problems. Sometimes we need to know rather than guess.

Here is the owners manual for my car. (*Page through the book.*) It tells what kind of gas and oil my car uses. The manual tells the correct way to start the engine and what to do if I get a flat tire. Without this book, I would have to guess how to care for my car. I don't want to guess because mistakes can be expensive.

What if you had to guess about what God expects of you? What if you guessed wrong? That would be frightening! But listen to what the prophet Micah said in today's Bible reading. (*Read the text.*)

Micah says that three things please God:

1. Act justly
2. Love mercy
3. Walk humbly

Maybe we should spend a few moments on each of those things. First, do you know what God means by acting justly? *Just* means "correct." So acting justly means doing what is right. For example, pretend your friend just got what you always wanted—a super-duper Whizmo. You would like a Whizmo of your own, and you're tempted to take it from your friend. Will you steal it? Probably not. You know it's wrong to steal even if you want something very much, so you act justly—correctly.

Loving mercy also pleases God. Loving mercy means showing kindness and forgiveness. Here's another story. Suppose Aaron borrows your crayons to work on his Sunday school project. Aaron is messing around with Allison and he breaks your favorite crayon in half. Would you demand that Aaron replace one broken crayon with a brand new box of 654 colors by sundown Sunday evening? Probably not. God expects us to forgive just as He forgives us.

Do you remember the third way of pleasing God? Walking humbly. Listen to this story. Renee was one of those kids who seemed to have everything. She was so friendly and kind that almost everyone liked her. She was pretty, too. Renee always wore neat clothes and usually got all her math problems correct. If Renee walked humbly, would she say, "Hey you. Make sure you sit far away from me. I'm too good for you"? Probably not. Walking humbly means not bragging about the blessings God gave you. Instead, what would you do with those blessings? (*Invite answers.*) Using your blessings to help others and to serve God are ways of walking humbly.

Rules, rules, rules. How can you remember them all? You probably can't. But when you make choices or decide how to act, remember that God gave an example of how to please Him. He sent Jesus to show and tell us how to act.

Let us pray.

Prayer. Dear Jesus, thank You for taking away my sins and giving me the power to please God. Give me the chance to show and tell others about Your love every day. Amen.

31

Every Day
in Every Way _____

EPIPHANY 5: Is. 58:5–9a; 1 Cor. 2:1–5; Matt. 5:13–20

Text. Is it not to share your food with the hungry and to provide the poor wanderer with shelter—when you see the naked, to clothe him, and not to turn away from your own flesh and blood? Then your light will break forth like the dawn, and your healing will quickly appear; then your righteousness will go before you, and the glory of the LORD will be your rear guard. *Is. 58:7–8*

Teaching aids. A hymnal, a Bible, and a five-dollar bill.

Gospel nugget. God gave us the Gospel to share with others.

Let's sit in rows like we do in church. (*Arrange the children, if necessary.*) We'll begin with a prayer, but it's proper to stand (*kneel*) while praying. Let's stand up (*or kneel*) to show respect to God.

Let us pray. Heavenly Father, thank You for bringing us together in worship. Give us ears willing to listen and hearts ready to accept all the love You give us. We pray in Jesus' name. Amen.

Be seated. We're going to learn something about worship today. We already learned that it's good to stand (*or kneel*) while praying to show respect for God. We can do several other things while worshiping.

This is a hymnal or songbook. (*Indicate the book.*) How do we use this in worship? (*Invite answers.*) That's right. We sing prayers and praise to God.

This is part of our worship service, too. (*Show the five-dollar bill.*) Our gifts to the Lord are collected during the offering. How is the money used? (*Encourage responses.*) The church uses money to pay its bills, and it also sends money to missionaries and others who preach and teach God's Word.

What is the most important part of worship? If you guessed God's Word, you're correct. (*Indicate the Bible.*) The Bible is the center of everything we do in church. The sermon is about something written in the Bible. And, of course, we hear readings directly from the Bible each Sunday. Today's readings were from the Bible books of Isaiah, First Corinthians, and Matthew. All three readings suggested ways to worship God. Let's listen again to two verses from Isaiah. (*Read the text.*)

Those verses don't describe our worship service, do they? Isaiah said that worshiping God is much more than going to church, singing hymns, saying prayers, and giving money. Oh, those things are very important, and God wants us to do them. But God wants more. God wants us to worship Him by everything—that's right, everything—we do. Does that mean we must always carry our Bible and keep our hands folded? Not really. Let me explain.

Who gets an allowance? How can you worship God when you get your allowance? (*Invite responses.*) You can save some of your allowance for the offering on Sunday.

One more example. Suppose you saw an accident between two cars. You probably don't know first aid, but there is a way you can help—and worship at the same time. Any ideas? (*Invite responses.*) We can pray for anyone injured in the accident, even if we don't know them. Everything we do can show we love others just as God loves us.

Let's pray for God's help in finding ways to worship Him.

Prayer. Dear Lord, You gave us faith and hearts that love You. Help us know how to worship You every day in every way. In Jesus' name. Amen.

What Will You Decide?

EPIPHANY 6: Deut. 30:15–20; 1 Cor. 2:6–13; Matt. 5:20–37

Text. This day I call heaven and earth as witnesses against you that I have set before you life and death, blessings and curses. Now choose life, so that you and your children may live and that you may love the LORD your God, listen to His voice, and hold fast to Him. For the LORD is your life. *Deut. 30:19–20*

Teaching aids. Any container for liquid that has poison warnings or symbols for poison (e.g., bleach, ammonia, etc.), and a milk or other drink container.

Gospel nugget. Having given faith, the Lord allows people to make choices.

Do you make many decisions? For example, do you decide what to eat for dinner? Can you pick which clothes to wear? Are you allowed to choose which TV programs to watch? Do you sometimes make bad choices?

Today's message is about decisions. I brought two containers, which I've placed before you. This bottle contains (*name the poisonous product*). How is this product used? (*Encourage responses.*) This material is definitely not for drinking. It's so dangerous that a special warning appears on the bottle. Look. (*Show the poison warning or symbol.*)

Next, we have a milk carton. Many people drink milk. Why? (*Encourage responses.*) Milk is safe for most people, and it makes strong bones and teeth. If you had to choose one of these items (*indicate the containers*) for lunch, which would you pick? The only good choice is milk.

The Bible talks about choices, or decisions, too. Did you hear the Old Testament reading? It said, (*read the text*).

In some ways, choosing to love God, listening to His voice, and holding fast to Him are like the decision you made moments ago. You have only one good choice. But sometimes making the right choice is difficult.

We all want to love, obey, and stay close to God, but sometimes sin gets in the way. Sin tempts us to make bad decisions. I think you might know something about this. Have you ever decided not to say your prayers because it was too much work or took too much time? That's not choosing God, is it?

Have you ever whined and complained and moaned and groaned about getting up for church—so much that Mom or Dad gave up and said, "Okay, stay in bed?" If that happens, it's deciding against God.

God's people are always free to make decisions. He gives people faith to believe in Him. But He allows us to use or to throw away that faith. In Old Testament days, some of God's people decided that God wasn't good enough for them. They chose to worship idols—statues that looked like cattle or people. They threw away their faith. It was a life-or-death decision—and they chose death.

I doubt that you pray to idols, but we sometimes love someone or something more than we love God. That's a bad choice. In our two examples about praying and being too lazy to worship, we would love ourselves and what we want more than we love God and what He wants. We thank and praise God that He forgives even those kinds of sins! Let's talk to God about that right now.

Prayer. Dear God, thank You for leaving us free to decide what to do with our faith. Forgive us when we make bad choices. Make us strong in faith so that we always choose You. In Jesus' name we pray. Amen.

Throw Away Your Halo

EPIPHANY 7: Lev. 19:1–2, 17–18; 1 Cor. 3:10–11, 16–23; Matt. 5:38–48

Text. The LORD said to Moses, "Speak to the entire assembly of Israel and say to them: 'Be holy because I, the LORD your God, am holy. ... Do not hate your brother in your heart. Rebuke your neighbor frankly so you will not share in his guilt. Do not seek revenge or bear a grudge against one of your people, but love your neighbor as yourself. I am the LORD.' " *Lev. 19:1–2, 17–18*

Teaching aid. A halo fashioned from a coat hanger or wire (or a picture of a saint with a halo).

Gospel nugget. Through Jesus Christ we are enabled to obey God's command of holiness.

I brought along a halo this morning because of the Old Testament reading. Part of it says, "Be holy because I, the LORD your God am holy." When I first heard those words, I thought, "We better get our halos out." (*Hold the halo to your head.*) How else can we be holy?

Do halos really make us holy like God? We know better. No one can be as holy as God until they get to heaven. But Jesus gives us power to live holy lives, and God the Father tells us how to use Jesus' power.

I want to reread part of the Old Testament lesson for today. Listen carefully, and you'll discover some ways to be holy. (*Read the text.*)

First, God told people why they should be holy. He didn't say, "Be holy because you'll get a better allowance." He didn't say, "Be holy so everyone thinks you're wonderful." God said to be holy because *He* is holy. Since God is God, I guess that's a good enough reason to be holy!

Next, God said, "Do not hate your brother in your heart." If you hate someone in your heart, you might never say the words "I hate you," but you would think and feel hate just the same.

God also tells us to help people see their sinful behavior and let them know that Jesus will forgive them. For example, imagine that you're playing with some friends. They find some matches and sneak behind your crabbiest neighbor's house. They begin striking the matches and holding them against his wooden garage. If something like that occurs, tell your friends they are wrong. God does not want us to make others suffer. Then urge your friends to ask God's forgiveness.

Avoiding revenge is another way to be holy. Revenge means getting back at someone for what they did. It's too bad that getting revenge is more popular than forgiving. We see revenge all around us. Maybe you've been riding in the car with Mom or Dad when another car followed close behind, horn honking loudly. The driver wants your car to go faster! Finally the car pulls out, passes, and then comes very, very, very close to hitting your car as it pulls in front of you. That's revenge!

The last part of today's message contains words that you've probably heard before. God says, "Love your neighbor as yourself." In other words, treat others as you like to be treated. That's a hard job. But we have help. When Jesus died to take away our sins, He made us holy. Holy means "without sin." But it's so easy to stop being holy! When that happens, Jesus wants us to ask forgiveness and take more of His power. Who needs a halo when we have Jesus' power? (*Toss the halo aside.*)

Go now and be holy as God is holy. Jesus will bless you with His power.

Still Following the Star

Text. Shout for joy, O heavens; rejoice, O earth; burst into song, O mountains! For the LORD comforts His people and will have compassion on His afflicted ones. ... See, I have engraved you on the palms of My hands; your walls are ever before Me. *Is. 49:13, 16*

Teaching aids. Attach a piece of adhesive tape with a star drawn on it to the palm of your hand, or draw the star directly on your palm with erasable ink. (Beware of sweaty palms!) Arrange to have an offering basket and a Bible in different locations around the church.

Gospel nugget. God sent Jesus to save, comfort, and transform sinners.

Today is the last Sunday in the Epiphany season. Do you remember what happened at the first Epiphany? (*Encourage responses.*) Epiphany is when the Wise Men followed a special star in the sky that marked the place where they found Jesus and worshiped Him.

I drew a star in the palm of my hand to help us worship today. (*Reveal the star.*) Wherever my hand goes, that's where we will find a way to worship Jesus. Would you follow my hand and me on a little journey around the church? Okay, let's go! (*Hold your hand up so you and the children can see the star. Lead the children to someone sitting at the end of a row.*)

We show we know Jesus when we're friendly to others, so I'm going to shake this person's hand and be friendly. (*Greet the person by name and say, "It's good to see you."*) Can you be friendly to some people today? Come on. Let's find some people to whom we can say good morning and shake their hands. Pick some people at the end of the rows. (*Demonstrate and encourage the children to participate.*) My, you are friendly today. But let's get together again and follow the star elsewhere. (*With your hand held in front, lead the children to an offering basket.*)

A basket (*plate*)? Why would the star lead to a basket? Perhaps we should find out how the church uses these baskets. Does anyone know? (*Encourage responses.*) Yes, we use baskets to receive money offerings.

Remember how the Wise Men brought valuable gifts to Jesus? We use baskets to gather valuable gifts for Jesus today. People put money in here to help the church tell about Jesus. But Jesus wants more than money from those who love Him. He wants us to sing, pray, and serve Him. People serve Jesus in church by playing musical instruments, teaching Sunday school and Bible class, handing out church bulletins, getting the altar ready for worship, and cleaning the church. When we know Jesus, we want to do as much as we can for Him.

Now it's time to follow the star again. (*Lead the children to the Bible.*) The Wise Men found Jesus living with His parents. Today we find Jesus living in the Bible. The Bible tells what God did for us and how we can please Him. One of today's Bible readings tells how God feels about us. (*Read the text.*)

The star in my hand reminds me about Jesus, but God has our names written in His hand to remind Him about us! And what does He think when He remembers us? He thinks, "Those are my kids. Jesus died to take away their sins and change their lives."

Let us pray.

Prayer. Dear God, thank You for making me Your own child. Help me find ways to show Your love to others. We pray in Jesus' name. Amen.

Solving the Mystery___

TRANSFIGURATION: Ex. 24:12, 15–18; 2 Peter 1:16–19 (20–21); Matt. 17:1–9

Text. The LORD said to Moses, "Come up to Me on the mountain and stay here, and I will give you the tablets of stone, with the law and commands I have written for their instruction." ... When Moses went up on the mountain, the cloud covered it, and the glory of the LORD settled on Mount Sinai. For six days the cloud covered the mountain, and on the seventh day the LORD called to Moses from within the cloud. To the Israelites the glory of the LORD looked like a consuming fire on top of the mountain. Then Moses entered the cloud as he went on up the mountain. And he stayed on the mountain forty days and forty nights. *Ex. 24:12, 15–18*

Teaching aids. A portable radio; a cross hidden beneath a piece of cloth and placed at a distance but within sight of the children.

Gospel nugget. Jesus was God's Son sent to take away the sins of the world.

I think we'll call today "Mystery Sunday." Would you help me solve some mysteries? Good. Let's start with an easy one. (*Show the radio.*) This radio is a mystery to me. I push a button (*turn it on*) and music or voices come out. I don't see anyone talking. (*Peer into the radio.*) I see no musicians performing the music. I can't figure out how sounds come from this radio. Can anyone help me? (*Invite responses.*) The sounds come from invisible radio waves floating through the air and into the radio.

Our next mystery involves God and Moses. You heard about it in today's Old Testament reading. God picked Moses to lead the children of Israel on their great escape from the Egyptians. Moses remained Israel's leader after the escape, too. One day, God called Moses up onto a mountain. It was so mysterious. Clouds surrounded the mountain so no one on the ground could see what happened to Moses. Then the clouds cleared away to reveal the top of the mountain—on fire! Poor Moses! What would happen? Do you know? (*Invite responses.*)

Moses didn't die on that fiery mountain. He met God, who showed His mysterious power with clouds and flames. And God had a special gift for His people. It was the Ten Commandments.

Today we celebrate another mystery, and it, too, happened on a mountain. Thousands of years passed after God's people received the commandments. The commandments were impossible to obey, and God knew His people needed help. So He sent a mysterious baby who grew into a mysterious man. The man was very good, so good that He perfectly obeyed all God's commands. A few loyal men and women listened to this man and believed what He said. They were called disciples. Two disciples climbed a mountain with Him, and a mysterious voice told them who this man was. A symbol for Him is under that cloth (*point to the cloth covering the cross*). Who was He? (*Encourage responses.*) Let's uncover the symbol to see if you're right. Yes, it was Jesus.

Many mysteries surround God. We'd like to know how He made the world and how He did His other miracles. But the most important thing about God isn't a mystery. He loves us.

We pray.

Prayer. Lord God, thank You for sending Jesus to make us Your people. Help all those who don't know You to solve the mystery of how they can be Your people. In Jesus' name. Amen.

Ashes, Crumbs, and the Bread of Life___

ASH WEDNESDAY: Joel 2:12–19; 2 Cor. 5:20b–6:2; Matt. 6:1–6, 16–21

Text. Then the LORD will be jealous for His land and take pity on His people. The LORD will reply to them: "I am sending you grain, new wine and oil, enough to satisfy you fully; never again will I make you an object of scorn to the nations." *Joel 2:18–19*

Teaching aids. Before the presentation, prepare some burnt toast. Also bring a slice of bread, a dinner plate, and a small trash container.

Gospel nugget. Repentance through faith in Jesus repairs lives destroyed by sin.

See this bread? (*Show the burnt toast.*) It's ruined. (*Crumble the bread or ashes in your fingers onto the dinner plate.*) Nothing but crumbs and ashes come from this burnt toast.

Speaking of ashes, today is Ash Wednesday. Why does this day have such a strange name? (*Encourage responses.*) Ash Wednesday begins a time of year called Lent. During Lent we remember how sin ruined our lives.

Ashes are a symbol or sign of sin—doing what God doesn't like or not doing what God likes. Some people smear ashes on their foreheads to show they are sinners. Are you a sinner? (*Encourage responses.*) Don't worry. I'll not rub ashes on your head. We'll imagine that the crumbs and ashes on this plate are sins. Whenever we do wrong, it's like making our lives into ashes and crumbs. Good for nothing but the trash. (*Place the crumbs into the trash container.*)

Many years ago, God's people felt like they were good for nothing but the trash. We heard about them in today's Bible reading from Joel. But God didn't want people to feel like worthless crumbs and ashes. God invited them to repent. (*When people repent, it means they are sorry for their wrongdoing and want to do better.*) Joel tells what happened after God's people repented. (*Read the text.*)

What does it mean that the Lord took pity on His people? (*Encourage responses.*) Yes, He felt sorry for them, and He promised to care for them. In a way, He changed their crumby ashes—and our crumby sins—into fresh lives, (*place the bread on the plate*) just like I am replacing the crumby ashes of bread with fresh bread.

How did God take away our worthless sins? (*Invite responses.*) That's correct. He sent Jesus. Did you know that Jesus called Himself the Bread of Life? He meant that He was all that anyone needed if they wanted to live with Him forever. Jesus makes us like fresh bread, too. Because He took away our sins, we can share His life-giving love with others. How might we feed Jesus' love to others? (*Invite responses.*) Telling others that Jesus died to take away their sins is one good way of sharing the Bread of Life. Treating others kindly and forgiving those who make us unhappy are other good ways of sharing the Bread of Life, too.

Let's ask and receive God's forgiveness right now. We'll work together on this prayer. I'll say part of the prayer, and when I lift the bread plate, you say, "Dear God, hear us." (*Practice the cue several times.*)

We are like ashes, Lord. (*Cue.*) We often do things You don't want us to do. (*Cue.*) We often don't do the good that You want us to do. (*Cue.*) Take pity on us, Lord, for we are miserable sinners. (*Cue.*) Forgive us, we pray, for the sake of Jesus, who died to take away our sins. (*Cue.*) Amen.

God forgives you. May He give you power to avoid sinning again.

It Started with Dirt___

LENT 1: Gen. 2:7–9, 15–17; 3:1–7; Rom. 5:12
(13–16), 17–19; Matt. 4:1–11

Text. The LORD God formed the man from the dust of the ground and breathed into his nostrils the breath of life, and the man became a living being. Now the LORD God had planted a garden in the east, in Eden; and there He put the man He had formed. And the LORD God made all kinds of trees grow out of the ground—trees that were pleasing to the eye and good for food. In the middle of the garden were the tree of life and the tree of the knowledge of good and evil. *Gen. 2:7–9*

Teaching aids. A handful of soil and a plate.

Gospel nugget. God created humans. He gives them all they need for life, both physically and spiritually.

Would you believe it? Scientists spend millions of dollars trying to figure out how life began on earth. You and I and this (*spread the dirt on a plate*) could answer their question for free.

Dirt. God's Word, the Bible, tells us life began with dust, or dirt. Listen to part of today's Bible reading. (*Read the text.*)

God created the first man from dust, or dirt. After creating Adam, God blessed him with many gifts. He gave Adam a beautiful garden home filled with fruit trees and other pretty plants. God also gave Adam a special helper. Her name was Eve. What a great home they had in the Garden of Eden!

God told Adam and Eve to use everything in the garden—everything except the fruit from one tree that would harm them. Can you imagine what kinds of fruit they ate? But Adam and Eve made one big mistake. They ate the harmful fruit. Adam and Eve disobeyed God, and by disobeying God they sinned.

44

Eve and Adam were the first sinners, but they certainly weren't the last. You and I disobey God even though He gives us everything we need for life. Sin dirties up our lives.

We could go on and on talking about the many ways to sin, but that would make us unhappy. I think we're ready for some good news. God found a way to clean up all the dirt caused by sin. No, it's not a vacuum cleaner. God sent Jesus to clean up sinners.

Today is the first Sunday in Lent. During Lent we think about what we have done and what God has done. Who has done better, God or us? Of course, God always does best. From the first man and woman on earth to the baby born in some hospital just moments ago, all people are sinners. They are just like dirt. But God sent Jesus to wash away our sins. He washed away our sins with His own blood—the blood He lost while dying on the cross to save us. Today, Jesus still washes away our sins—and He doesn't even need water. When we ask Jesus to forgive us for all the wrong we do, He says, "Worry no more. I forgive you. Be happy and strong and faithful."

Please pray with me. Lord Jesus, thank You for giving us what we need most—forgiveness. Keep us faithful forever. Amen.

Now you may go. But remember, Jesus wants to hear about your sins, and you can be sure He'll forgive you. Be happy and strong and faithful.

Read the Big Print___

LENT 2: Gen. 12:1–8; Rom. 4:1–5, 13–17;
John 4:5–26 (27–30, 39–42)

Text. The LORD had said to Abram, "Leave your country, your people and your father's household and go to the land I will show you. I will make you into a great nation and I will bless you; I will make your name great, and you will be a blessing. I will bless those who bless you, and whoever curses you I will curse; and all peoples on earth will be blessed through you." *Gen. 12:1–3*

Teaching aids. A warranty or guarantee card from an appliance or other product; a large piece of poster board on which is written in large letters *I WILL ALWAYS LOVE YOU. YOU WILL LIVE FOREVER.*

Gospel nugget. God is faithful to His promises, including the promise of salvation.

Have you made any promises lately? What were they? (*Invite responses.*) Will you keep your promises? I hope you do.

This card (*show the warranty*) contains promises. It explains what the makers of my (*mention the product*) will do if it stops working. Look at this card. Why is it difficult to read? (*Invite responses.*) Yes, the print is very small—so small that I haven't read it carefully even though it promises something to me. I believe when you make a promise, you should do it in big, loud letters that everyone can read and trust.

God made His promises big and bold. Listen to the promises He gave Abram. (*Read the text.*)

Do you think Abram trusted God to keep His promises? Why? (*Encourage responses.*) Yes, God loved Abram.

Abram trusted God even though God asked Him to do some-

46

thing very difficult. God told Abram to get all his stuff together and leave home. Would you leave home if God told your family, "Get up and go?" It would be hard, but Abram knew that God would never let Him down.

Let's take a closer look at God's promises to Abram. God said, "I will make you into a great nation and I will bless you." God meant that a large and strong group of people would someday be Abram's relatives. When Abram died many years later, he did have a large family.

God made another promise to Abram. "I will make your name great, and you will be a blessing." Thousands of years after Abram died, people still knew who he was. Even Jesus' disciples knew Abram was a friend of God.

God's last promise to Abram was also a promise to us. God said, "All peoples on earth will be blessed through you." God kept that promise by making Jesus one of Abram's relatives.

God makes big and bold promises to us, also. (*Indicate the poster board.*) God says, "I will always love you." We can believe God's promise. God will always love us because He sent Jesus to take away our sins. No matter how bad we might be, God always wants us to say, "I'm sorry I did wrong. Please forgive me." God never runs out of forgiveness.

God says, "You will live forever." He will keep this promise, too. When we Christians die, we go right on living in heaven with Jesus. Let's thank God for His promises.

Prayer. Dear God, thank You for keeping Your promises. We especially thank You for Jesus, who promised to come and take us to our new home in heaven. Amen.

Smoothing Out the Bumps

LENT 3: Is. 42:14–21; Eph. 5:8–14; John 9:1–41 or John 9:13–17, 34–39

Text. I will lead the blind by ways they have not known, along unfamiliar paths I will guide them; I will turn the darkness into light before them and make the rough places smooth. These are the things I will do; I will not forsake them. *Is. 42:16*

Teaching aids. A toy on wheels or a ball; about six hymnals placed in a row, but with various angles and gaps between them.

Gospel nugget. God promises never to forsake the faithful on their journey to meet Him.

I hope you're ready to solve a problem this morning. I want to move this toy (*ball*) from the beginning of these books to the end. But as you can see, my hymnal highway isn't in good shape. It has rough places where the toy would fall off. Can you solve this problem? (*Allow the children to arrange the books into a smooth path.*) Thank you. (*Move the toy along the "road."*) The rough road is now smooth.

Sometimes being a Christian is like this toy on our hymnal highway. All kinds of bumps and gaps and twists keep us from getting close to Jesus. But today's Old Testament reading has some welcome words for Christians. Listen. (*Read the text.*)

The Bible says that God takes care of us and that He will always take care of us. Let's see what that means. Suppose that one night you are so frightened and worried that you can't sleep. Why? During the day you got so mad at Mom that you yelled and screamed and said some nasty things you wish you hadn't said.

Now you're worried. You're afraid that neither God nor Mom will forgive you. But remember today's Bible passage. God said, "I will not forsake you." God means He will always forgive you when you're sorry. I think Mom also would forgive you if you said you were sorry.

Here's another example of how God cares for us. We know that really good Christians have wonderfully happy lives, don't they? They do? No, no, no. Are you always happy? Do you think I'm happy all the time? Things sometimes go wrong even though we are Christians. For example, several people on today's prayer list are sick or suffering. (*If possible, mention the names of those who requested prayers at this service.*) When people are ill or unhappy, God listens to their prayers. God wants us to pray for ourselves and for others who are feeling hurt, sick, or afraid. He says, "I'll make the rough places smooth." God comforts people when life gets rough and they trust Him to make things better.

God is certainly good. He knows our needs, and He will help us no matter what happens. Let's thank God for His goodness and ask Him to make our rough places smooth. Please pray with me by repeating the words I say.

Prayer. Dear God, ... Thank You for promising ... never to forsake us. ... We trust You ... to always be with us ... no matter what happens. ... Remind us to talk with You ... anytime we're worried ... or frightened ... or sick ... or sad. ...Forgive our sins ... and help us obey You. ... Heal the sick ... and make the weak strong. ... We pray in Jesus' name. ... Amen. ...

Countdown_____

LENT 4: Hos. 5:15–6:2; Rom. 8:1–10; Matt. 20:17–28

Text. Come, let us return to the LORD. He has torn us to pieces but He will heal us; He has injured us but He will bind up our wounds. After two days He will revive us; on the third day He will restore us, that we may live in His presence. *Hos. 6:1–2*

Teaching aids. The numerals 3, 2, and 1 written on separate index cards; know the number of days until your birthday, Good Friday, and Easter Sunday.

Gospel nugget. The resurrected Jesus assures us of forgiveness.

It's only _____ more days until my birthday! Do you know how many days are left until your birthday? (*Allow responses.*)

Let's try an easier one. How many days remain until Good Friday? (*Reveal the number.*) Okay, and that makes it only __ more days until Easter. I don't know about you, but I like to count down the number of days left until very special days. In fact, I like counting down for all kinds of reasons. Would you play a countdown game with me? I have three cards marked 3, 2, and 1 (*show the cards*) to help us count down.

Let's count down from three to one. After we get to one, you stand and shout "Praise the Lord." Ready? Let's count. 3 ... 2 ... 1 ... Praise the Lord! Very good.

Would you like to do a few more? When we get to one, show how you feel when you sin—when you do things that God doesn't like. (*Each child may do different things.*) Let's count. 3 ... 2 ... 1 ... action. (*Allow the children to express verbally or nonverbally their feelings.*) Wow. It looks like you feel sad or maybe scared

50

when you do something wrong. I don't want you to feel that way, so let's hurry and do another countdown. Show how you feel knowing that God forgives when you sin. Let's go. 3 ... 2 ... 1 ... action. (*Allow time for expression.*) What a difference! God's forgiveness makes us happy.

You remind me of some words Hosea the prophet wrote in today's Old Testament lesson. Listen. (*Read the text.*)

God's Old Testament people often wandered away from Him. They thought they didn't need to obey or worship or pray. God's people forgot Him until they really needed Him badly. When sinning caused trouble, they remembered God's promise to be their powerful helper. Then they prayed and trusted God to help.

I think something was missing in that Bible passage I read moments ago. I think something was missing in our countdown game, too. Something was missing between feeling bad about doing wrong and receiving God's forgiveness. Do you know what we forgot? We overlooked saying that we were sorry. I think Hosea's people made the same mistake.

Often we're sorry for doing wrong because we get caught or because we feel guilty. The real reason for feeling bad about our sins is that sins keep us away from God. We want to be close to God, don't we? Besides feeling bad about our sins, we also need to honestly say, "Dear God, I'm sorry I did wrong. Help me do better next time." Then we can be sure God will give us power to hate doing wrong and love doing good. That makes me feel like one more countdown—our "Praise the Lord" countdown. Ready? 3 ... 2 ... 1 ... Praise the Lord!

Come to Life_____

LENT 5: Ezek. 37:1–3 (4–10), 11–14; Rom. 8:11–19; John 11:1–53 or John 11:47–53

Text. I will put my Spirit in you and you will live, and I will settle you in your own land. *Ezek. 37:14*

Teaching aid. A simple hand puppet. If none is available, make one by gluing several pieces of yarn to the top of a work glove or a sock. Use markers to make eyes and nostrils. Let the thumb form the lower jaw and the fingers form the upper face of the puppet. Move your thumb to simulate puppet-talking. (*Consider recruiting someone to work with you. Save the puppet for use on Pentecost 24.*)

Gospel nugget. The Holy Spirit gives life through the sacrifice and victory of Jesus.

(*The puppet is in a limp heap on the floor.*)

Presenter: I wanted to use a puppet for this morning's message, but it isn't doing anything. It's just a lifeless heap on the floor. I'll give the message without it unless you have some suggestions. (*Encourage responses.*)

I see. I should put it on my hand. Okay, let's put some life into this puppet. (*Put the puppet on your hand.*)

(*The puppet silently looks at the presenter.*)

Presenter: Why don't you say something?

Puppet: What do you want me to say?

Presenter: Say good morning to the boys and girls.

Puppet: Good morning boys and girls! How are you today? You look so nice this morning. I'm happy you came to church.

Presenter: I just said to say good morning. Don't overdo it.

Puppet: Well, you put me in a friendly mood. I'm no ordinary puppet, you know. I need someone to get me started, but once I come to life, well, look out!

Presenter: Great. In some ways, you're just like real, live Christians.

Puppet: Christians are puppets?

Presenter: No, but they do need someone to get them started and keep them going.

Puppet: Who brings them to life?

Presenter: God the Holy Spirit makes them come to life. The Holy Spirit makes ordinary people into V.S.C.s.

Puppet: What's a V.S.C.?

Presenter: A V.S.C. is a Very Special Christian. Every Christian is very special. God sent His Son to take away the sins of all people, and the Holy Spirit gives people faith to believe this great news.

Puppet: I see. Those who believe Jesus saved them are Very Special Christians.

Presenter: That's right. And V.S.C.s do and say what God wants them to do and say.

Puppet: Kind of like I do with you, huh?

Presenter: Yes, but people can refuse to believe in God and do His will. You puppets don't have such a choice.

Puppet: That's silly. Even a puppet like me would want to believe that Jesus took away his sins.

Presenter: Some people refuse to believe. I guess they think doing God's will is too much like being a puppet. But if we don't let the Holy Spirit guide and help us, we're just like those dry bones we heard about in today's reading. Dead. They were dead until something special happened. Would you read it again?

Puppet: Sure. It's from the book of Ezekiel. (*Read the entire Old Testament lesson—Ezek. 37:1–14.*)

Presenter: Did you hear that? "I will put my Spirit in you and you will live." That's what God said.

Puppet: I get it! The Holy Spirit brings Christians to life. And Christians want to thank God by doing what He wants them to do.

Presenter: You got it. (*To the children.*) And you got it, too. Go with the Spirit.

Brave for Jesus _____

**PALM SUNDAY: Is. 50:4–9b; Phil. 2:5–11;
Matt. 26:1–27:66 or Matt. 27:11–54**

Text. It is the Sovereign LORD who helps me. Who is he that will condemn me? They will all wear out like a garment; the moths will eat them up. *Is. 50:9*

Teaching aid. An article of old, tattered clothing, cloth, or rag.

Gospel nugget. God strengthens His people to face afflictions.

Ah, Palm Sunday. What a special day for the church! Even if you know the Palm Sunday story, it's good enough to hear again and again. I think of it as the Jesus Parade.

Jesus was on His way to Jerusalem. Many people loved Jesus, and others just wanted to see Him—perhaps meet Him. People lined the road, waiting for Him to pass. As Jesus went by, they shouted, "Hosanna! Blessed is He who comes in the name of the Lord. Hosanna in the highest!" They were happy to greet and meet their Savior.

The days following Palm Sunday weren't nearly as happy for Jesus and His friends. Jesus ate His last meal with the disciples. One of them, Judas, told Jesus' enemies where they could capture Him. Jesus' enemies took Him to court and demanded that He be killed. They said that Jesus claimed to be God, and they didn't believe He was God. Jesus died on the cross within a week of His great parade. Of course, the story doesn't really have a sad ending. Be sure to come back next week and celebrate Easter—the day Jesus came back to life.

For now, we need to think and learn about Palm Sunday. Let

me ask a few questions. First, who are you more like—the people who welcomed Jesus or the people who killed Him? (*Encourage responses.*) Most of us compare ourselves with those who shouted happy hosannas during the parade. Okay, now a second question. Has anyone ever made fun of you because you believe in Jesus or because you go to church or Sunday school? I hope not, but that happens to Christians like you and me.

It happened to Isaiah, God's prophet in the Old Testament. Today's Bible reading told how Isaiah felt. He said that he didn't care who made fun of him or threatened him. Isaiah said, "Even if they pull out my beard [ouch!] because I believe in God, I don't care. God will take care of me. They can hurt me, but they can't keep me from talking about God. They can hurt me over and over and over until they wear out like this piece of cloth (*reveal the cloth*), tattered, worn out, eaten by moths!" What Isaiah really meant was that his enemies would wear out long before he would give up his love for God. And God would help him through all his troubles.

Jesus wasn't always treated well either. His parade was great, but many people would rather argue with Him than worship Him. They called Him a liar, and they shouted "Crucify Him! Crucify Him!" instead of "Hosanna in the highest." Yet Jesus trusted God the Father, and He did what God expected of Him. He saved you and me.

Let us pray.

Prayer. Dear God, thank You for giving us faith in Jesus and for being our friend. Help us be brave for You. We pray in Jesus' name. Amen.

Finally Right _____

EASTER: Acts 10:34–43; Col. 3:1–4;
John 20:1–9 (10–18) or Matt. 28:1–10

Text. Then Peter began to speak: "I now realize how true it is
that God does not show favoritism but accepts men from every
nation who fear Him and do what is right. You know the message
God sent to the people of Israel, telling the good news of peace
through Jesus Christ, who is Lord of all." *Acts 10:34–36*

Teaching aids. A stuffed Easter bunny, an Easter basket, and
a colored egg (*or pictures of them*).

Gospel nugget. Jesus Christ defeated sin and death.

Happy Easter! The best thing about Easter is the Easter
bunny. (*Indicate the bunny.*) Right? No? Okay then, the best thing
about Easter is an Easter basket. (*Indicate the basket.*) Right? Not
right again, hmmm. Then the best thing about Easter must be colored Easter eggs. (*Indicate the egg.*) Right? Wrong again. I haven't
been right yet, so I better let you tell me. What is the best thing
about Easter? (*Encourage responses.*)

Jesus rose from the dead on the first Easter. He came back to
life although His closest friends, the disciples, never expected to
see Him again. What a wonderful surprise!

When the disciples realized that Jesus was really God, they
wanted to keep the news a secret so no one else would be saved.
Right? I'm wrong again? Who does Jesus want to know about Him?
(*Encourage responses.*) Let's check the Bible to see if you're right.
I believe the book of Acts tells us. (*Read the text.*)

Yes, indeed, you're correct. Jesus died to save all people, so
everyone needs to know their Savior. Right? Whew. It feels good to
be right once in awhile.

Our Bible verses said that Jesus accepts all people who do what is right. Am I right or wrong? Does Jesus love you only when you obey all the commandments? (*Pause for response.*) Wrong? I'm glad I was wrong about that one. If Jesus loved only those who were perfect, Easter would be very sad. It is faith that makes us right with God for Jesus' sake.

Here is another statement. You tell me if I'm right or wrong. Jesus loves only those who deserve to be saved. (*Pause for response.*) Wrong again? You mean that Jesus died to save sinners? (*Pause.*) Yes, you *are* right. Do you know whom Jesus helped while He lived on earth? He helped sinners—sinners who knew they needed help. So He went to people like tax collectors, who cheated people. He went to "unclean" people like those sick with leprosy. Jesus went to people that nobody liked and people that others feared.

Are you a sinner? Everyone in this church is a sinner. Sometimes we don't do what God expects. Sometimes we do what God doesn't like. Sometimes we sin without even knowing it.

Is Jesus here with us sinners? Of course, He is. He still comes to sinners. And when Jesus comes to us sinners, He shouts and screams and hollers because we're so bad. Right? Wrong again. Jesus listens when we tell Him we are sinners. Then He forgives us again and again and again. And each time He forgives, He also gives us power to hate sin. Sin killed Jesus. But He is more powerful than sin. He came back to life. And after we die, we'll come back to life, too. Then we'll live with Jesus, and we'll never be wrong again. Right? Right! Finally right. Happy Easter.

Somebody
Had to Pay_____

**EASTER 2: Acts 2:14a, 22–32; 1 Peter 1:3–9;
John 20:19–31**

Text. This man was handed over to you by God's set purpose and foreknowledge; and you, with the help of wicked men, put Him to death by nailing Him to the cross. But God raised Him from the dead, freeing Him from the agony of death, because it was impossible for death to keep its hold on Him. *Acts 2:23–24*

Teaching aid. Bill from an electric company or other company.

Gospel nugget. God sent Jesus to pay for our sins.

(*Act sad or concerned.*) Ah, good morning children. (*Look at the bill.*) I'm so concerned about this bill that I'll have a hard time keeping my mind on today's message. This is the electric bill for our church (*or home*). It's kind of high, but it's really no surprise. Each time we turn on a light switch or operate the furnace (or air conditioning) we use electricity. The organ uses electricity and so do the machines in the office. We used the electricity, and now we must pay for it. Maybe some generous person will pay the bill. But maybe not.

This electric bill reminds me of the Bible reading from Acts that you heard earlier. Peter was telling people about Jesus. He said, (*read the text*).

Sometimes we think it was a bad mistake that Jesus died on the cross. The Bible says that although He did nothing wrong, He was accused of a crime and killed for it. But the Bible also says, "[Jesus] was handed over to you by God's set purpose." In other words, Jesus' death was no mistake or accident. God purposely sent Jesus to die on the cross. Sounds cruel, doesn't it?

When people sin, God says, "You're not living the way I told you to live. Now you must pay for your sins." If we think this electric bill is high, just think about the bill for our sins! We couldn't pay it. Neither could anyone else. So God, because He loves us so much, decided to help. God decided that Jesus could pay for the sins of everyone in the world. During the last few weeks we heard how Jesus did that. He lived a perfect life. He did nothing wrong. Jesus obeyed all the commandments, and, even better, He truly loved God the Father and all the people on earth. He lived the kind of life God wanted all people to live. Jesus lived perfectly because Jesus was God.

Since someone had to pay for our sins, Jesus did it Himself. That's like the electric company paying for the electricity they supplied and we used! It's unlikely to happen. Nobody loves us like God loves us. Jesus paid for our sins with His suffering and death.

And now for the Good News we heard so clearly last Sunday. Jesus isn't dead anymore! On the third day after Jesus paid for our sins, He came back to life. Jesus rose from the dead. He's with us right now, and He'll stay with us wherever we go. He took away our sins, and someday He'll also take us to heaven.

Though Easter Day is over, I don't think we ever want to forget the Easter Good News. So let's wish everyone a Happy Easter. Ready? Let's do it. (*Lead the children.*) Happy Easter!

What Shall We Do?

EASTER 3: Acts 2:14a, 36–47; 1 Peter 1:17–21; Luke 24:13–35

Text. "Therefore let all Israel be assured of this: God has made this Jesus, whom you crucified, both Lord and Christ." When the people heard this, they were cut to the heart and said to Peter and the other apostles, "Brothers, what shall we do?" Peter replied, "Repent and be baptized, every one of you, in the name of Jesus Christ for the forgiveness of your sins. And you will receive the gift of the Holy Spirit. The promise is for you and your children and for all who are far off—for all whom the Lord our God will call." *Acts 2:36–39*

Teaching aids. A pot with a cover; two bowls.

Gospel nugget. Jesus saved us from our sins and fills us with the Holy Spirit.

What foods are cooked in pots? (*Encourage responses. Use soup as an example to continue the story.*) I'm glad you mentioned soup because I have a sad story about soup, this pot, and two children named Bill and Relma. (*Remove the cover from the pot.*) As you can see, the pot is empty. All the soup is gone but not because it was eaten. The soup pot is empty because Bill and Relma had an accident.

Mom decided to make Bill and Relma's favorite soup, cream of chicken. The children smelled the soup warming, and they could hardly wait for Mom's call to lunch. In fact, they couldn't wait. Bill, being older and taller, took the soup pot from the stove (*demonstrate, holding the pot by its handle*) and carried it to the table. Relma got two soup bowls (*indicate the bowls*) and placed them on the table. Bill began pouring (*demonstrate*) the soup into the bowls. The pot felt heavier and heavier so Bill poured faster and faster until ... whoops! (*Tip the pot all the way over to simulate a spill.*) Cream of chicken all over the table! Mom would be very angry. Relma began crying. What could she and Bill do? Maybe they could hide the spilled soup. No, it wouldn't be right to fool Mom. Besides, how can you hide soup that's slopped all over the table? They considered saying, "Mom, we have no idea how that soup spilled. Maybe it was aliens or something!" They decided Mom was too smart to believe that story. What do you think they should do? (*Invite responses.*)

People are often frightened when they do something wrong. In Relma and Bill's case, they were wrong in not waiting for Mom to serve the soup. But all of us have more serious problems. Take the group Peter talked to in today's Bible story from Acts. Listen. (*Read the text.*)

Peter had excellent advice. He told them to repent and get baptized. Through Baptism, the Holy Spirit makes us God's children—or even God's grown-ups. Repenting is like reminding ourselves how much we need God. How do people repent? (*Encourage responses.*)

We do two things when we repent. The first is we admit we did something wrong. We tell God we're sorry for our sins. The second is we tell God that we want to do better. Shall we try that right now? Let us pray.

Dear God, we are sorry that we often disobey You. Make us strong so we can do better. We pray in the name of Jesus, who takes away our sins. Amen.

Isn't it great? Jesus not only forgives our wrongdoing, but He also fills us with the Holy Spirit so we live as forgiven and forgiving people. May the Holy Spirit make you stronger each day.

Do-it-yourself Project

EASTER 4: Acts 6:1–9; 7:2a, 51–60; 1 Peter 2:19–25; John 10:1–10

Text. So the word of God spread. The number of disciples in Jerusalem increased rapidly, and a large number of priests became obedient to the faith. *Acts 6:7*

Teaching aids. A slice of bread and some soft, easily spreadable margarine; a plate for the bread; a box with a cover; a table knife; a Bible.

Gospel nugget. God empowers Christians to spread the Good News.

This morning we'll start with an interesting project. I have some margarine and a slice of bread. I like margarine spread all over my bread so I'll put the margarine close to the bread and get ready for a snack. (*Move the margarine and bread next to each other and wait several seconds before proceeding.*)

Nothing happened. Somehow, some way, I'll get that margarine on my bread. Maybe the margarine is shy. I'll place the margarine and bread inside this box and cover it. There. While no one is watching, I'm confident the margarine will slather itself all over that delicious slice of bread. (*Wait several seconds before opening the box.*) Okay, get ready, tummy, here comes our favorite snack. (*Look inside the box.*) Uh oh. Look for yourself. Nothing happened.

I could take a knife, which I just happen to have, and spread the margarine on the bread myself. (*Demonstrate.*) That certainly got the job done! Spreading margarine on bread is a do-it-yourself project.

During the past few Sundays, our Bible readings have been from the book of Acts and have told how the first Christians told others about Jesus. About 2000 years have passed since the disciples first told others about Jesus. Yet, many people neither know Jesus nor believe in Him. They don't know how much Jesus loves them and that He died to take their sins away. We still need people to spread the Good News about Jesus. Let's do another project to discover the best way of telling others.

This might work. (*Hold the Bible high.*) Okay, Bible, you're God's Word. Do your thing. Go tell the whole world about Jesus. (*Wait several seconds.*) Is the Bible still up there? Hmmm. That may not be the best way of sending God's Word to others. Maybe God's Word likes to work in secret. (*Place the Bible in the box and cover.*) Let's wait a moment to see what happens. (*Pause. Then open box.*) Who wants to look first? (*Select a child.*) Is the Bible gone? No? God's Word does no good sealed in a box either.

Pray! Yes, pray. We could ask God to find someone who will spread His Good News. But what if God answers our prayer by choosing us? What can we do?

We can follow the example of Christians who lived around Jerusalem in those months following the first Easter. Today's Bible reading said that God's Word spread and more people became disciples. And those new disciples told others about Jesus who then told others who then told others who then told others—well, I think you get the idea. God wants us to spread the Good News ourselves. If any friends or relatives don't know that Jesus loves them, you can spread the margarine—I mean the Good News.

Prayer. Dear Jesus, thank You for giving us the Good News. Make us brave when we have a chance to tell others about You. Give us power to make spreading the Good News a do-it-yourself project. Amen.

Friends

EASTER 5: Acts 17:1–15; 1 Peter 2:4–10; John 14:1–12

Text. As his custom was, Paul went into the synagogue, and on three Sabbath days he reasoned with them from the Scriptures, explaining and proving that the Christ had to suffer and rise from the dead. "This Jesus I am proclaiming to you is the Christ," he said. Some of the Jews were persuaded and joined Paul and Silas, as did a large number of God-fearing Greeks and not a few prominent women. But the Jews were jealous; so they rounded up some bad characters from the marketplace, formed a mob and started a riot in the city. They rushed to Jason's house in search of Paul and Silas in order to bring them out to the crowd. But when they did not find them, they dragged Jason and some other brothers before the city officials, shouting: "These men who have caused trouble all over the world have now come here, and Jason has welcomed them into his house. They are all defying Caesar's decrees, saying that there is another king, one called Jesus." When they heard this, the crowd and the city officials were thrown into turmoil. Then they made Jason and the others post bond and let them go. As soon as it was night, the brothers sent Paul and Silas away to Berea. On arriving there, they went to the Jewish synagogue. *Acts 17:2–10*

Teaching aid. A piece of colored yarn tied like a bracelet around your wrist or any item a friend gave you.

Gospel nugget. Jesus is our best friend, who shelters and empowers us.

What gifts have you received from friends? (*Encourage responses.*) A friend gave me this friendship "bracelet" (*or other item*). Isn't it neat? It reminds me how much my friend and I like each other.

How do friends treat each other? (*Invite responses.*) Friends treat each other well. They help when you have problems, and they enjoy spending time with you. Friends do not always agree with each other, but they know how to forgive and how to get along.

Friends are important. Jesus had 12 close friends called disciples. He had other good friends, too—people like Mary, Martha, and Lazarus. These friends shared their love with Jesus and with each other. After Jesus went to heaven, His friends told new friends about Him. This is how the Good News that Jesus saved sinners spread around the world.

One of today's Bible readings told about several friends who traveled from town to town, telling others about Jesus. Paul and Silas stayed at a friend's house. They all got into trouble and needed help. Listen to what happened. (*Read the text.*)

It sounds like Paul and Silas had as many enemies as friends. While Paul and Silas taught others about Jesus and made new friends, they also made new enemies. Fierce enemies—wicked enemies—who started trouble. Their enemies also threatened a friend of Paul and Silas. But did you hear what happened? Friends rescued Paul and Silas, helping them escape in the dark night. They also kept Jason out of jail. Now those are good friends!

Have any friends rescued you? (*Invite responses.*) We all have one special friend who rescued us, and I think you know His name. Our friend is Jesus. He rescued us from our enemy the devil.

Let us pray.

Prayer. Dear Jesus, You are our best friend. We love You and pray that we'll be as faithful to You as You are to us. Amen.

God Is Close-by_____

Text. From one man He made every nation of men, that they should inhabit the whole earth; and He determined the times set for them and the exact places where they should live. God did this so that men would seek Him and perhaps reach out for Him and find Him, though He is not far from each one of us. "For in Him we live and move and have our being." As some of your own poets have said, "We are His offspring." *Acts 17:26–28*

Teaching aid. Hand-holding.

Gospel nugget. God gives us life and remains close-by.

Are we sitting close enough to hold hands? Let's hold each others' hands (*demonstrate*) and begin with prayer.

Dear God, come close to us now and give us a stronger faith. Help us listen and learn and praise You this morning. We pray in Jesus' name. Amen.

Okay, you can let go of your neighbors' hands. We held hands while we prayed. At what other times might people hold hands? (*Encourage responses.*)

It's comforting to hold hands when we're scared. We feel safe when we hold hands with Mom or Dad as we cross the street or when we're in a large crowd. Sometimes people hold hands just because they like each other. One thing is true no matter who you're holding hands with—the other person must be within reach. You certainly can't hold hands with anyone across the room.

Do you think God is close enough for holding hands? Let's see what the Bible tells us. (*Read the text.*)

Today's Bible reading says that God is near us. That's good news because we need God's love and care. God knows where we are and what we need at all times. It's like God is holding our hand. But sometimes we don't want to hold His hand. Close your eyes and imagine this story.

You and God are good friends—such good friends that you're holding hands with Him. Now, you know that God is stronger and smarter and better than your other friends. But, once in awhile, you would rather not be so close to your best friend—like the time Mom told you to turn off the TV and come to dinner. God tugged on your hand and said, "C'mon. Let's get to the table." After God said that, you pulled your hand free from His and remained snuggled in the soft chair watching your favorite cartoon. The next time Mom called, her voice was angrier and louder and you were in trouble. Whose fault was it, yours or God's? Of course, it was your own fault. God was pulling you in the right direction, but you pulled yourself free.

Even when we refuse to hold hands with God, He always remains close-by, waiting for us to reach for Him. We reach for God's hand when we're sorry about disobeying Him. We reach for God's hand when we're sick, in trouble, or just plain scared. And God reaches back. He takes our hand and says, "I forgive you, and I'll always be here for you." If you're sick or frightened, God says, "Take my hand. I'll protect you. Even when you die, I'll bring you to life again and we'll live in heaven forever."

Let's close by joining hands again and praying.

Prayer. Dear God, thank You for loving us and holding our hands. Help us reach out to others in love and kindness, too. Amen.

Get Rolling

EASTER 7: Acts 1:(1–7) 8–14; 1 Peter 4:12–17; 5:6–11; John 17:1–11

Text. But you will receive power when the Holy Spirit comes on you; and you will be My witnesses in Jerusalem, and in all Judea and Samaria, and to the ends of the earth. *Acts 1:8*

Teaching aid. A ball.

Gospel nugget. God equips and enables Christians to witness to His glory.

Do you enjoy playing ball? I do. That's why I brought along this ball to help with today's message. (*Place the ball in front of the children.*) I wonder if this ball is equipped with batteries? (*Inspect the ball.*) No, there's no place for batteries. Perhaps an engine makes it roll. (*Inspect the ball again.*) No, I don't see a place to provide gas for an engine. Maybe it has a string attached. (*Inspect the ball again.*) Nope. No string. Tell me, how do you get a ball rolling? (*Invite responses.*)

You must push, throw, or kick a ball to get it moving. Does a ball ever quit rolling on its own? Of course, the ball will stop by itself unless someone keeps pushing or throwing or kicking it.

We Christians are like a ball. We need a push to get us rolling. (*Demonstrate with the ball.*) The early Christians were like that, too. Today's Bible reading from Acts tells how they got rolling.

The disciples were speaking with Jesus, and they wanted to know what He would do next. He had already died on the cross and come back to life. Now He was about to enter heaven, but He didn't want to leave the disciples feeling lonely and powerless. So Jesus made this promise: (*Read the text.*)

The Holy Spirit would get the disciples rolling, but rolling where? Their job was to witness. Witnesses tell what they've seen. Who had these disciples seen? (*Invite responses.*) Yes, they had seen Jesus. They had also seen the many wonderful things Jesus had done for others. The best thing they had seen was Jesus come back to life after dying for our sins.

Where were the disciples to witness? Jesus sent them to the whole world! The disciples needed lots of power to do their witnessing. The Holy Spirit rolled them from place to place, spreading the good news about Jesus. Many people believed the witnesses, so many people became Christians.

Now all this took place about 2000 years ago. Talk about a longtime to keep a story rolling! You and I hear the same message that people heard when the disciples first began witnessing. The Holy Spirit keeps adding more and more believers to Jesus' family. Will people 2000 years from now need this message? They surely will! How can we keep the Good News rolling until then?

We have the same power that pushed the first Christians into sharing the message. The Holy Spirit lives in us, so we have the gift of faith, too. What story can you tell? (*Invite responses.*) That's right. Be ready to tell all who will listen that Jesus took away their sins. They can believe this story because it's God's own words from the Bible.

You can use the Holy Spirit's power when you get older, too. Someday you may teach Sunday school or become a pastor or teacher (DCE, deaconess, etc.). And if you become a mom or dad, you can tell your kids the good news you already know. Then they'll tell their kids who will tell their kids who will tell their kids—for another 2000 years—or more!

Go now and roll with peace and power! Amen.

Team Spirit_____

PENTECOST: Joel 2:28–29; Acts 2:1–21; John 16:5–11

Text. And afterward, I will pour out My Spirit on all people.Your sons and daughters will prophesy, your old men will dream dreams, your young men will see visions. Even on My servants, both men and women, I will pour out my Spirit in those days. *Joel 2:28–29*

Teaching aids. A patch, pennant, clothing, or other item with the logo of a local sports team. Also, a dove symbol (Holy Spirit) and a match or lighter.

Gospel nugget. The Holy Spirit fills us with faith and equips us to share the Gospel.

(*Substitute the team of your choice.*) What is your favorite sports team? (*Encourage responses.*) The Chicago Bulls are mine. Would you like to see my Bulls pennant? (*Show the pennant, etc.*) This symbol shows that I'm a Bulls' fan. I get really excited while watching the Bulls. Sometimes I feel like I'm part of the team. I think that is called "team spirit."

God's people had a very special team Spirit. They had symbols to show their team Spirit, too. Here is one of their symbols. (*Indicate the dove either as a symbol displayed in church or cut from a piece of paper.*) The dove is a symbol of the Holy Spirit, and today is the Spirit's special day.

Today is *Pentecost*. On the first Pentecost, Jesus' disciples were together when they heard what sounded like a strong wind. Then they saw another symbol of the Holy Spirit. (*Light the match or lighter.*) Little flames of fire danced above their heads. The Holy Spirit was giving the disciples a team spirit. But team spirit for

70

what? Basketball? Baseball?

Jesus' disciples needed team spirit for the most important job anyone can do. With the Holy Spirit's help, these disciples could tell others that Jesus took away the sins of the world.

Now this team of disciples was no ordinary team. They were champions! The Holy Spirit made them able to speak many languages. Why would the disciples need to speak languages other than their own? (*Invite responses.*) Yes, the disciples met people from all over the world. The disciples had to speak languages that others understood. The Good News about Jesus spread around the world. Now the Holy Spirit and His team of disciples were even world champions! We are part of the Holy Spirit's team, too. Do you think you have team spirit? The prophet Joel says you do. Listen. (*Read the text.*)

Jesus poured His Spirit on us and made us a good team. We are good because Jesus took away our sins. That makes us actual players on the Jesus team—on the world-champion Jesus team. Your job is to tell others about Jesus. And your job is to do what Jesus did—love others (even those who are hard to love), forgive others, and do good for others. You can do it. After all, you have the holy team Spirit!

Please pray with me.

Prayer. Dear Holy Spirit, thank You for speaking my language. I'm ready to work on Jesus' team. Fill me with love, goodness, and bravery so that I say and do things that make others want to join Your team. Amen.

Very Good

THE HOLY TRINITY: Gen. 1:1–2:3; 2 Cor. 13:11–14; Matt. 28:16–20

Text. God saw all that He had made, and it was very good. And there was evening, and there was morning—the sixth day. Thus the heavens and the earth were completed in all their vast array. *Gen. 1:31–2:1*

Teaching aids. An apple or other fruit with seeds; a knife to cut open the fruit.

Gospel nugget. God created all things and continues to care for His creation.

Do you ever wonder where things come from? I do, so I brought along an apple to help us wonder where apples come from. Let's see if we can trace their history.

Where do you think I bought this apple? (*Invite responses to all questions.*) Very good. I got the apple at a grocery store. The grocer bought the apple from an orchard. What kind of plant grows apples? Very good. Apples grow on apple trees. But do you know how apples become apples on trees? They begin as flowers, and the flowers change into apples.

We know apples grow from flowers on trees, but where do apple trees come from? Very good. Apple trees grow from seeds. Where do the seeds that grow apples come from? Very good. (*Cut open the apple to reveal its seeds.*) The seeds that grow apple trees that produce flowers that turn into apples come from … apples! Just think, when God created apple trees, He found a marvelous way to keep apples growing for thousands of years. Very good, God!

Let's talk about people now—people like you and me. Where

did you come from? Very good. We all came from a mom and dad. And where did Mom and Dad come from? They came from a grandma and grandpa. And Grandma and Grandpa came from a great-grandma and great-grandpa. God certainly has a "great" way of keeping people on earth, doesn't He?

God not only keeps the earth filled with good things, but He also cares for all creation. Oh, there was a time when God destroyed nearly every living thing on earth. The world was filled with wicked people who hated God. He noticed that His very good creation wasn't very good anymore. God wanted to wipe out the evil people, so He sent a flood over the whole earth. But God also loved His creation, so He saved some of every animal on an ark built by a faithful man named Noah. He also saved Noah's family, who believed in God.

After the flood, Noah's family grew larger and larger. Plants began growing, as they do after floods. The animal families grew larger, too. Soon thousands of people lived on earth again. God loved the people, including you and me, so much that He sent Jesus to take away our sins. Very good, God! And after Jesus took away our sins, God sent the Holy Spirit to help us remain His people and serve Him. Very good again, God! Isn't it fantastic how God takes care of us? He forgives our sins and keeps us close to Himself. Someday, we'll meet every other Christian in heaven, and I think we'll hear God say, "Very good. I'm glad you're here. Meet Jesus. He's the one who made you good enough to be with Me. And meet the Holy Spirit, too. He gave you faith and kept you faithful."

I think we might say something back to God. How about "Very good, God?" Can we say those words together? Ready? Set? Go. Very good, God.

Amen.

Make a Note of It____

PENTECOST 2: Deut. 11:18–21, 26–28;
Rom. 3:21–25a, 27–28; Matt. 7:(15–20) 21–29

Text. Fix these words of Mine in your hearts and minds; tie them as symbols on your hands and bind them on your foreheads. Teach them to your children, talking about them when you sit at home and when you walk along the road, when you lie down and when you get up. Write them on the door frames of your houses and on your gates, so that your days and the days of your children may be many in the land that the LORD swore to give your forefathers, as many as the days that the heavens are above the earth. *Deut. 11:18–21*

Teaching aids. Five sheets of note paper. Print one word per note sheet: *Jesus took away your sins.* Before the service, attach the notes in sequence to five locations in the nave where you will take the children.

Gospel nugget. God provides us with His saving Word.

Please remain standing this morning. In a moment we'll take a walk to hunt for five important messages. Before we look for the notes, I'd like to reread some of today's Old Testament lesson for your parents. You see, this morning's message for you is also a message for them. Can you see your parents out there? Why don't you wave to them? Now watch to see if they listen while I read. (*Read the text.*)

Were they listening? Were you listening? Good. Let's walk this way. (*Lead the children toward the first note.*) Tell me when you see a note.

Here is the first note, and it contains only one word. Who will read the word? (*Choose a volunteer to read each note.*) *Jesus.* The

74

first word we found is *Jesus.* Let's move on and look for the second word. (*Lead the children.*) Tell me when you see it.

There it is! The second note also has one word. Who will read it? The second word is *took.* Now we have two words, *Jesus took.* Onward, children! (*Lead the children.*) Keep your eyes peeled for a third note. Tell me when you see it.

We found note number three. Who will read it? The third note contains the word *away.* Putting our three words together we now have *Jesus took away.* Note number four is next. (*Lead the children.*) I believe I see it up ahead. Let's look at what it says. (*Show the note and invite a child to read it.*) The fourth word is *our.* So far we have *Jesus took away our.* What did Jesus take that was ours? (*Invite answers.*) We'll see if you're correct when we find the fifth note. Back to the trail! (*Lead the children.*) Tell me when you see it.

The fifth note has the word *sins. Jesus took away our sins.* This is the message God wants our parents and us to remember. God's message is so important that He wants people to make notes and place them everywhere possible. God's notes can be placed on your hands and forehead, on doorways and gates, near your bed and in your car, and just about every other place. Make some notes when you get home.

Now, will you pray with me?

Prayer. Dear God, thank You for giving us words that remind us of Your love. Help us remember those words always. Thank You for sending Jesus to take away our sins. Give us power to hate doing wrong and to love serving You. We pray in Jesus' name. Amen.

Detour

PENTECOST 3: Hos. 5:15–6:6; Rom. 4:18–25; Matt. 9:9–13

Text. "Then I will go back to My place until they admit their guilt. And they will seek My face; in their misery they will earnestly seek Me." "Come, let us return to the LORD. He has torn us to pieces but He will heal us; He has injured us but He will bind up our wounds. After two days He will revive us; on the third day He will restore us, that we may live in His presence." … "For I desire mercy, not sacrifice, and acknowledgment of God rather than burnt offerings." *Hos. 5:15–6:2, 6*

Teaching aid. Make a *DETOUR* sign, preferably black letters on an orange background (to add authenticity).

Gospel nugget. God reveals our sinful nature and invites us to receive forgiveness in Christ.

Do you have your driver's license yet? No, of course not. But I think you already know some things about road signs.

Pretend you're riding along a road when suddenly you see this. (*Indicate the sign.*) Dad says, "Detour shmeetour! I don't see any road work. We'll just ignore the sign. Two miles later, your car bounces wildly on broken concrete. Three flat tires later, Dad says, "I'm sorry I didn't go around this mess. Now I'm really in trouble."

Detour signs often make travelers unhappy. When they detour, it means they can't go the way they want to go. But detours show safe ways around dangerous places.

Did you know that God uses detour signs, too? Here's how His detour signs work. Suppose it's only a half hour until suppertime. Heather is hungry, so she asks Dad for some potato chips. He says, "No potato chips right now. We'll be eating soon." Then Dad leaves

76

the room, so Heather sneaks into the kitchen, quietly opens a bag of potato chips, and stuffs her mouth full over and over again. Heather feels "funny" about her behavior, so she slips the potato-chip bag into the cabinet. Dad returns and never suspects that Heather was nipping the chips. Whew! She got away with it. Nobody but Heather knows the wrong she did. Nobody but Heather. And God.

"Supper is served," calls Dad. Heather takes her seat at the table and nibbles tiny bits of food. Dad asks, "What's wrong?" She answers, "I'm not hungry."

"Not hungry?" cries Dad. "Why, half an hour ago you couldn't wait to eat. Are you sick?" he asks. About this time Heather begins to feel very guilty, so she tells Dad about the potato chips—and how sorry she is for disobeying him.

God's detour sign was at work even though Heather ignored it at first. God warns us not to sin, and He doesn't let us get away with it. Something always happens when we do wrong—even if we think we got away with it. In the case of the smuggled potato chips, Heather's stomach got full, and she felt guilty about fooling Dad. Feeling guilty is like seeing a gigantic detour sign. (*Indicate the sign.*) Detour. You can't always do what you want. You must go around the wrong thing, and do the right thing. God will help you detour dangerous sin. He wants you to detour and do things His way.

Let's thank God for helping us detour around sin.

Prayer. Dear God, thank You for letting us know what is wrong and reminding us to detour around wrongdoing. Thank You for keeping us safe from sin. Amen.

Keeping Promises____

PENTECOST 4: Ex. 19:2–8a; Rom. 5:6–11; Matt. 9:35–10:8

Text. " 'You yourselves have seen what I did to Egypt, and how I carried you on eagles' wings and brought you to Myself. Now if you obey Me fully and keep My covenant, then out of all nations you will be My treasured possession. Although the whole earth is Mine, you will be for Me a kingdom of priests and a holy nation.' These are the words you are to speak to the Israelites." ... The people all responded together, "We will do everything the LORD has said." So Moses brought their answer back to the LORD. *Ex. 19:4–6, 8*

Teaching aid. An empty milk carton or other product container.

Gospel nugget. God keeps His promises even though His people don't keep their promises.

What promises have you made? (*Encourage responses.*) When you make promises, people expect you to keep them. But do you always keep your promises?

Promises remind me of this carton of milk. I just bought it at the grocery store. When I get a carton of anything, I expect it to be full. Buying a closed container is like getting a promise. The store promises that this container is full of milk. But look at this. (*Open the carton and hold it upside down.*) Nothing. The carton was empty. The store's promise of a full carton was empty, too. Empty promises!

Listen to God's Word from the book of Exodus. (*Read the text.*) I heard two promises there. First, God promised to make the children of Israel His very, very special people *if* they perfectly obeyed Him. Second, the children of Israel promised to obey God perfectly. That sounds fair. Do you think God kept His promise? (*Wait for responses.*) Do you think the children of Israel kept their promise?

The children of Israel's promise was like this carton of milk. Empty. At first they wanted to obey God, but they failed miserably. Are we ever like that? Sadly, we are.

Did God keep His promise to the children of Israel? Remember, He said, "If you obey Me, I'll take special care of you, and you will be My special people." God kept His promise even though His people failed. God was kind and good. He found someone who would keep their promise for them.

God did the same for us. We want to be His children, but we can't do what is necessary. We don't always love God perfectly. Some of us might use God's name the wrong way by cursing or swearing. We even use God's name wrong when we say "Oh God." Cursing, swearing, and saying "Oh God" whenever we please are ways that show we don't love God perfectly.

We can't love other people perfectly either. But God expects us to be perfect. He has every right to throw us out of His family because we don't obey Him. But God is also good. Remember? He sent someone to obey His laws for us. Who was that someone? Yes. Thank God for Jesus!

Jesus kept all the promises we couldn't keep. He takes away our sins and makes us perfect in God's sight. We must go to Jesus each day and tell Him that we need Him. We need His forgiveness to make us perfect over and over and over.

Please pray with me.

Prayer. Dear Jesus, we admit we aren't perfect. Thank You for being perfect for us. Help us hate sin and do what is right. Amen.

Good Medicine_____

Text. Sing to the Lord! Give praise to the Lord! He rescues the life of the needy from the hands of the wicked. *Jer. 20:13*

Teaching aid. A bottle of over-the-counter medication such as cough medicine or acetaminophen (substitute *headache* for *cough*).

Gospel nugget. Jesus rescues His children from sin.

I once had a friend named Lisa who thought she found a way to keep from getting coughs. She went to the drug store and bought some cough medicine. (*Show the bottle.*) Lisa carried that bottle of medicine wherever she went. My friend thought the medicine bottle would keep her from getting sick.

My friend was wrong. One day she woke up with a loud, hacking cough. Lisa was so disappointed with the cough medicine that she wanted to throw it away. But I said, "Lisa, cough medicine will help you when you have a cough. Don't throw it out. Take a teaspoonful and you'll feel better." Lisa listened to me. Soon her cough was gone. Cough medicine to the rescue!

The story about Lisa and her cough medicine reminds me of God and one of His friends, a prophet named Jeremiah. To Jeremiah, I think God was like Lisa's bottle of medicine. Now, Jeremiah was a faithful believer in God, and God made Jeremiah like a preacher or pastor. Jeremiah probably hoped that faith in God would give him a happy life free from any trouble. But Jeremiah's enemies had other ideas. They hated him and did things to hurt him.

God said, "Jeremiah, believing in Me doesn't mean you will

escape fears and tears and pain. Believing in Me may not bring you lots of friends or money or good health. But because you and I are friends, I'll help you when you're afraid, sad, hurt, lonely, poor, or sick. I'll come to your rescue. You and I will be friends forever."

You see, God was like good medicine for Jeremiah. He didn't keep trouble away from Jeremiah, but He did help when Jeremiah was in trouble. Jeremiah was so delighted with God that he cheered, (*read the text*).

Like Jeremiah, we sometimes hope God will keep us perfectly happy. But God allows us to get sick or sad and lonely or mad. And although He sent Jesus to take away our sins, we still suffer, and we still do some bad things. But Jesus is ready to help. He rescued us from the devil. And even if we die, Jesus rescues us and takes us to heaven where we we'll always be happy and healthy.

Please pray with me. Say the words "Jesus to the rescue!" each time you hear me say, "Who will help?" (*Practice several times before proceeding. Invite the congregation to join you.*)

Prayer. Oh Lord, sometimes we have very bad days. *Who will help? (Response.)* Even though You gave us families, sometimes we wish they would love us more or treat us better. *Who will help? (Response.)* We get coughs, colds, and the flu. And some of Your faithful people get cancer and AIDS. *Who will help? (Response.)* You forgive our sins, but we keep on sinning. *Who will help? (Response.)* Remind us of You and Your love for us. Then we'll always know *who will help. (Response.)* Sing to the LORD! Give praise to the LORD! He rescues us from the hands of the wicked. *Who will help? (Response.)* Amen.

The Whole Truth_____

PENTECOST 6: Jer. 28:5–9; Rom. 6:1b–11; Matt. 10:34–42

Text. But the prophet who prophesies peace will be recognized as one truly sent by the LORD only if his prediction comes true. *Jer. 28:9*

Teaching aids. A pencil and tablet or other paper.

Gospel nugget. God revealed His truth and kept His promise of salvation through Jesus Christ.

(If you're comfortable doing so, talk and act like a slick magician.) Hurry on down, young folks. Take a seat here if you want to be dazzled by tricks never seen before. You'll delight in the treats I'm about to pull from thin air—or rather from thin pencil. *(Indicate the pencil.)* Yes, I'm about to make this pencil, this ordinary pencil, change into wonders limited only by your imagination. Is everybody ready? Well, what are we waiting for?

I can make this pencil *do* anything—*be* anything you want. What would you say if I changed this pencil into a frothy, large root-beer float? You would like that, wouldn't you? Is there anything you would like more? *(Encourage responses and make a list on the paper.)*

Let's ask the adults what they would like. Who would like a sleek, red sports car? How about 10 million dollars? Anyone for a lifetime of happiness? Yes, I can do it all.

(Pause. Normal voice.) But before I forget why I'm really here, I better read a Bible verse to you. I believe it comes from the book of Jeremiah, the bad news/sad news prophet. Aha, here it is—Jeremiah 28:9. *(Read the text.)*

Now if that sounds like a strange Bible verse to you, you're not alone. Why did Jeremiah say you can only trust someone who says he has a message from God if that message comes true? Jeremiah was a prophet. God told him what to say, and Jeremiah said it. But many people didn't like what God said. Naturally, they didn't like Jeremiah either. You see, God's people didn't obey Him very well. They did what they wanted instead of what He wanted. So God punished His people by letting a wicked king make them prisoners. Jeremiah told them life would be hard and miserable. This is not what the people wanted to hear, so they listened to someone who had a happier message. His name was Hananiah, and he promised that everything would be okay. That's when Jeremiah said, *(repeat the text)*.

If you were prisoners kept by an evil king, whose message would you prefer, Hananiah's or Jeremiah's? Hananiah's message never came true. In fact, Hananiah died a prisoner.

A few moments ago I told you I would turn this pencil into *(consult and read list)*. You would really be happy if I could do that. But I can't. I'm as much a false magician as Hananiah was a false prophet. I know you're disappointed, but I do have some entirely truthful and happy promises for you.

Promise number one: Jesus took away your sins. Jesus didn't need magic because He is God and God can do anything. How do we know this is true? The Bible tells us, and the Bible is always right!

Promise number two: Someday you will live with Jesus in heaven. Do you believe that promise? Why? *(Invite responses.)*

We believe Jesus tells the truth. And although people get sick and die or killed in accidents, they will come back to life and live with Jesus forever.

Let us pray.

Prayer. Dear Jesus, thank You for saving me. Help me tell this Good News to everyone I meet. Amen.

Not What Some Expect

PENTECOST 7: Zech. 9:9–12; Rom. 7:15–25a; Matt. 11:25–30

Text. Rejoice greatly, O Daughter of Zion! Shout, Daughter of Jerusalem! See, your king comes to you, righteous and having salvation, gentle and riding on a donkey, on a colt, the foal of a donkey. *Zech. 9:9*

Teaching aids. A glass of water, a communion wafer, and a Bible, each in a separate closed box.

Gospel nugget. The Holy Spirit builds uncommon faith with common tools.

These three boxes contain what everyone needs.

The first box contains a liquid. If you could have any drink you wanted right now, what would it be? (*Invite responses.*) When we think of drinks, our favorites might be orange juice, milk, or some soft drink. But inside this box, I have the best liquid. (*Open the box and remove the glass of water.*) Water! Yes, water might not taste as good as our favorite drink, but most of our favorite drinks contain lots of water. Speaking of water, how is it used in our church? (*Invite response.*)

People are baptized with water. Baptism might not look like anything special, but a miracle takes place every time someone is baptized. The miracle is that God makes baptized people His very own children!

Moving on to our next box, I have the world's best food inside. What is your favorite food? (*Encourage responses.*) I have truly the greatest food right in this box. (*Reveal and remove the com-*

munion wafer.) It's probably not what you expected. This is a communion wafer. Older people in our church go to Holy Communion where they eat this wafer and drink some wine. In ways that only God understands, the wafer is also Jesus' body and the wine is also Jesus' blood. Another miracle! Jesus Himself started Holy Communion. He said that Communion brought forgiveness of sins.

This third box contains the most important information in the world. People may look in dictionaries, encyclopedias, almanacs, atlases, or computer programs when they want information. But this box contains only one book. Can you guess which book? Of course, it's the Bible. (*Remove the Bible from the box.*) Who wrote the Bible? God put His words in the Bible, though He used people like Moses, Zechariah, Matthew, and Paul to write His words.

In today's Old Testament reading, we heard what God told Zechariah to say. Listen. (*Read the text.*)

Zechariah lived long before Jesus arrived on earth. He told others what to expect from the Savior whom God promised. Many people expected some great king to swoop down with a mighty army, destroying every enemy of God's people. But Zechariah didn't say what the people expected. He said Jesus would be humble and gentle.

The Bible tells us more about our Savior. He didn't take away our sins by wiping out the devil and his evil followers. Jesus did His job by dying on the cross. People didn't expect Him to do that! Then Jesus did something else few people expected. He came alive again!

We expect Jesus to return someday. Are you ready to meet Him? I know you are. We're ready because Jesus took away our sins.

Let us pray.

Prayer. Dear Jesus, we don't know when You're coming, but we're expecting You. Please come soon. Amen.

Every Second Counts

Text. As the rain and the snow come down from heaven, and do not return to it without watering the earth and making it bud and flourish, so that it yields seed for the sower and bread for the eater, so is My word that goes out from My mouth: It will not return to Me empty, but will accomplish what I desire and achieve the purpose for which I sent it. *Is. 55:10–11*

Teaching aid. A watch or clock

Gospel nugget. God's Word comforts, forgives, and strengthens us.

Who is good at telling time? (*Choose one child.*) Look at my watch, and tell me the time.

Very good. I'll try not to make this too long. Once in awhile we'll check the time, okay?

Is there anyone on whom you can always rely for help? (*Encourage responses.*) Mom and Dad are usually good for help. Police officers and fire fighters are good in dangerous situations. We count on our pastor (DCE, teachers, Sunday school teachers, etc.) for help, also. All these people are God's helpers. They are God's gifts to us. Let's check the time now. (*Check the watch.*) It's about 30 seconds later than when we last checked.)

God's Word is a lot like the helpers we mentioned a few seconds ago. We count on it to help us. Listen to part of today's Bible reading from Isaiah. (*Read the text.*)

Isaiah compared God's Word to the rain and snow. As you

probably know, rain and snow water the ground so trees, flowers, and crops can grow strong and healthy. God's Word works the same way, and it works every time. Whenever and wherever people hear God's Word, it goes to work and helps faith to grow.

Let's check the time again. (*Check the watch.*) About 60 seconds passed since we last checked. During that time, we listened to God's Word, and I told you about God's Word, too. God's Word makes us stronger second by second.

God's Word tells us some things we don't like to hear. For example, the Bible says that you and I are sinners. Bad news, huh? But remember Isaiah, who said that God's Word always does what it needs to do. Jesus died to take away our sins. We need to hear about our sins so we remember that only Jesus takes them away.

God's Word has good news, too. The good news goes right along with the bad news. In fact, you heard some good news moments ago when we declared that Jesus forgives our sins. Can the news get any better? It does. But let's check the watch again. We have spent another 60 seconds getting stronger on God's Word.

Jesus makes us friends with God forever. Do you think my watch can measure "forever?" I'm sure it can't. But we don't need watches to measure time when it comes to God's Word. His Word is always good, and we gladly hear it time after time after time as we live with Him both here on earth and later in heaven. God's Word in the Bible makes us stronger on earth. And when we go to heaven, we'll listen to God's very own voice with our very own ears. God's Word will make us happy forever. You can count on that!

We pray.

Prayer. Thank You for giving us Your Word, dear God. Make all who hear it stronger in faith. Give us strength to share Your Word every second of the day. Amen.

God's ABCs _____

Text. This is what the LORD says—Israel's King and Redeemer, the LORD Almighty: "I am the first and I am the last; apart from Me there is no God. … Do not tremble, do not be afraid. Did I not proclaim this and foretell it long ago? You are My witnesses. Is there any God besides Me? No, there is no other Rock; I know not one." *Is. 44:6, 8*

Teaching aids. An A and a Z cut from cardboard; a dictionary; a Bible marked at Eph. 2:1, 4–5, and 10.

Gospel nugget. God's care encompasses all of life.

We'll begin today's message with a couple of cheers, and we will use these letters (*indicate the A and the Z*) to help us. (*If the group of children is small, invite the congregation to participate.*) When I hold up the A and say "Give me an A," you say, "A." Let's try it once. Give me an A! (*Encourage the participants to respond.*) Now let's do the same with this letter. (*Indicate the Z.*) Give me a Z! Good. Now we are ready to do it for real.

Give me an A! (*Participants respond.*) Give me a Z! What does it spell? What does it spell? It spells *God!* You don't think so? Listen to part of today's Old Testament reading from Isaiah. (*Read the text.*)

God said He was the first and the last. When I think of the first and the last, I think of the beginning and the ending of the alphabet. What comes between the first and last letters? (*Invite responses.*) Of course, all the other letters. Just imagine, with only 24 other letters wedged between the A and Z, we can spell any word in our language. Let me demonstrate with this dictionary.

88

(*Open the dictionary to any page and choose a long word. Pronounce it and spell it.*) Did I use only letters from the alphabet? Certainly! (*Repeat the activity.*) Using only 26 letters we can spell any word, even if we don't know what it means.

Praise God that He is both the first and the last—like the A and the Z. If God is both the A and the Z, then He must also be like all the letters in between. God is good for everyone and everything. Instead of a dictionary that arranges 26 letters into thousands of words, God gave us a book that tells everything He did for us and what He wants us to do for Him. Can you name that book? (*Encourage responses.*) Yes, it is the Bible.

Let me demonstrate how the Bible helps us live. Ephesians 2:1 should help. (*Read the verse.*) Dead in our sins? That's what would happen if we had no one to save us. But God takes care of us. Listen to Ephesians 2:4–5. (*Read the verses.*) What great news! Doesn't it make you want to cheer? Give me an A! (*Pause for response.*) Give me a Z! What does it spell? God!

But wait a minute. Shouldn't we thank God for His love? Perhaps the Bible says something about that, too. Here it is. (*Read Eph. 2:10*)

Let's pray for power to do good works.

Prayer. Dear God, thank You for being everything we need. Give us the desire and the power to do good things in Your name. Amen.

More

PENTECOST 10: 1 Kings 3:5–12; Rom. 8:28–30; Matt. 13:44–52

Text. "Now, O LORD my God, You have made Your servant king in place of my father David. But I am only a little child and do not know how to carry out my duties. ... So give Your servant a discerning heart to govern Your people and to distinguish between right and wrong. For who is able to govern this great people of Yours?" ... So God said to him, "Since you have asked for this and not for long life or wealth for yourself, nor have asked for the death of your enemies but for discernment in administering justice, I will do what you have asked. I will give you a wise and discerning heart, so that there will never have been anyone like you, nor will there ever be." *1 Kings 3:7, 9, 11–12*

Teaching aid. A box of crayons; hold one crayon separately. (Alternative: A box of anything; adapt the message accordingly.)

Gospel nugget. God gives more than we ask.

I was drawing a picture the other day when I discovered I had no crayons. I didn't want to be greedy, so I asked my friend if I could borrow one crayon (*display one crayon*) to finish my project. She said, "Wait. I'll get what you need." Moments later my friend returned with this. (*Show the remaining crayons in their box.*) Wasn't she generous? I asked for only one crayon and she gave me the whole box!

Something similar happened to Solomon when he was the new king of Israel. Solomon was about 20 when he began ruling Israel. Now 20 years old might sound very old to you, but 20 is very young for someone to wisely rule a whole country. Solomon had special help, though. God appeared in a dream and promised to give Solomon whatever he wanted. Tell me, for what would you pray if God said, "Whatever you want, I'll give it to you?" (*Invite responses.*)

Solomon didn't ask for gold or jewels or expensive clothing. He didn't ask for things that would be good for him alone. You see, Solomon was worried. He wasn't sure he could be a wise and good king for God's people, so he asked God for help. Solomon used some fairly big words for a twenty-year-old, but I think you will understand. Let me read Solomon's prayer and God's answer. (*Read the text.*)

Solomon got more than what he asked. God promised to make him a king like no other. God gave him a wise heart. We remember Solomon as one of the wisest rulers who ever lived.

God still promises to answer prayers. The Bible says we will get whatever we ask in His name. Now, that doesn't mean we should expect a new bicycle or a million dollars just because we pray for those things. We need to pray wisely, like Solomon. Let's try a wise prayer right now. Repeat the words after me.

Dear God, ... we ask You ... to make us more like Jesus. ... Help us to love You more than anything. ... Help us to love other people, ... even those who don't love us. ... In Jesus' name we pray. ... Amen. ...

Prayers like that please God. God wants us to be good Christians. In fact, He wants us to be great Christians. And when God hears prayers for a stronger faith or for power to do good things, He answers by giving us more strength and more power than we ever imagined. God blesses His faithful and loving children. God bless you!

Free for All_____

PENTECOST 11: Is. 55:1–5; Rom. 8:35–39; Matt. 14:13–21

Text. Come, all you who are thirsty, come to the waters; and you who have no money, come, buy and eat! Come, buy wine and milk without money and without cost. Why spend money on what is not bread, and your labor on what does not satisfy? Listen, listen to Me, and eat what is good, and your soul will delight in the richest of fare. Give ear and come to Me; hear Me, that your soul may live. I will make an everlasting covenant with you, My faithful love promised to David. *Is. 55:1–3*

Teaching aids. Several grocery items representing nutritious food groups and "junk" foods

Gospel nugget. Faith and salvation are free and abundant gifts of the Holy Spirit through Jesus Christ.

Imagine you are walking by (*name a local grocery*) and you see a sign that says "free food every day." At first you might be suspicious. What store would give anything away without charging? But if the sign says "free" it must be free. You go inside to investigate, and you discover that the sign was honest. All the food prices are marked with zeroes! As you walk down the aisles, you see foods like these. (*Indicate the groceries.*) With which would you be tempted to fill your grocery cart? (*Encourage responses and ask why the children made their particular choices.*)
Some of you would fill your cart with (*name of junk food*). But milk, meat, bread, fruits, and vegetables are healthier foods. If all food were free, we could choose whatever we wanted and as much as we wanted. However, we would need to make wise choices to stay healthy and grow strong.

Our story about free food is only make-believe, but today's Old Testament lesson is real. Listen to Isaiah's announcement. (*Read the text.*)

When Isaiah mentions free milk, wine, and bread, he is using picture language to talk about gifts from God. All good things come from God, but His most valuable gifts are faith, salvation, and the Bible. Faith causes us to believe that Jesus is our Savior. Salvation means that Jesus saved each of us, and that He forgives our sins and wants us in His holy family. And the Bible is God's Word so we can read and hear what He did for us and what He wants us to do for Him. Faith, salvation, and God's Word—each is absolutely free for all people. You can have as much as you want, any time you want.

If God has these gifts for people, isn't it strange that sometimes we don't want His gifts? Like in our imaginary grocery store, sometimes we choose things that aren't good for us. That's called sin. Sin is an evil and deadly gift from the devil. The devil wants us to believe that hating God and doing bad things is better than loving and obeying God. Every time we do wrong, we choose gifts from the devil—gifts meant to harm us and keep us away from God. It's a good thing that God gives the gift of forgiveness! It's a good thing God never runs out of forgiveness because we need more of it than any other gift!

Let us pray.

Prayer. Dear God, sometimes it's hard to believe that You have so many gifts for us. Strengthen our faith so that we always remain close to You. Help us share Your gifts with all those around us. We pray in Jesus' name. Amen.

Reservations _____

PENTECOST 12: 1 Kings 19:9–18; Rom. 9:1–5; Matt. 14:22–33

Text. Yet I reserve seven thousand in Israel—all whose knees have not bowed down to Baal and all whose mouths have not kissed him. *1 Kings 19:18*

Teaching aid. A "reserved" sign from the church. Alternative: Make one from an index card folded the long way. Place the sign in the area where you will present the message.

Gospel nugget. God preserves His children to proclaim the Good News from generation to generation.

(*Indicate the "reserved" sign.*) Look at this. We have our very own place for today's message. The sign says "reserved." That means someone expected us, and made reservations for us. This space was reserved for us.

How else have you heard the word *reservation* used? (*Encourage responses.*) Adults may call for reservations at their favorite restaurant so a table is ready when they arrive. When people travel, they may reserve a hotel room so they're sure to have a place to sleep. Sports fans may buy reserved seats at the baseball park or football stadium. When something is reserved, it is kept aside for special people.

Perhaps you heard the word *reserve* in today's Old Testament lesson. God said He reserved 7,000 people of Israel. These were people who believed in God and worshiped only Him. At one time, many more than 7,000 people believed in God. But little by little that number dropped as people refused to worship Him.

Today, many more than 7,000 people believe in Jesus. We are among them, and God has special reservations for us. First, God reserved a special place for us. Where does each of us have reservations? (*Encourage responses.*) Yes, in heaven. And do you know who made those reservations? Jesus is the only one who can get us into heaven. He paid for the reservations, too, when He suffered and died for our sins. It's great knowing we have a wonderful place to live after we die. But we don't need to wait that long to enjoy other reservations God made for us.

God reserved a place on earth for Christians like you and me. Because Jesus died to take our sins away and make us holy, God reserved us to work for Him. How can people work for God? (*Invite responses.*)

We have at least two important jobs—telling others about Jesus and doing good things for others. God helps with both jobs by filling us with the Holy Spirit. When the Holy Spirit fills us with power, we know what to say about Jesus. Tell me what you can say about Jesus. (*Invite responses.*)

See, that's proof that God has already given you His Holy Spirit. If you know about Jesus and believe that He's your Savior, you have the Spirit's power to share that news with others.

Our second job is to do good deeds. Many of us enjoy doing good for others. We know the good that Jesus did for us by taking away our sins and making us friends with God. Now we can show others how much God loves us by loving others enough to treat them kindly, help them with their work, and forgive them if they treat us badly. Are you ready to work for God? Good. Go in peace. And remember, God reserved you to do His work.

God's Club

PENTECOST 13: *Is. 56:1, 6–8; Rom. 11:13–15, 29–32; Matt. 15:21–28*

Text. "These I will bring to My holy mountain and give them joy in My house of prayer. Their burnt offerings and sacrifices will be accepted on My altar; for My house will be called a house of prayer for all nations." The Sovereign LORD declares—He who gathers the exiles of Israel: "I will gather still others to them besides those already gathered." *Is. 56:7–8*

Teaching aid. Tickets—either homemade or leftovers from some event—many more than the number of anticipated participants.

Gospel nugget. God continues to bring people into His kingdom through Jesus Christ.

Please remain standing until I give each of you a ticket. I want to be sure we have room for all of you. These tickets show that you're members of God's Club. (*Distribute tickets.*) Okay, all of you ticket-holders may sit. (*Indicate the leftover tickets.*) I still have many more tickets, and we still have lots of room for more children. We can save these tickets for others who might join us later.

Our ticket situation reminds me of something God said to Isaiah and the children of Israel. Listen. (*Read the text.*)

The last sentence had especially good news. "I will gather still others to them besides those already gathered." That's like having lots of leftover tickets. (*Indicate the tickets.*) God always has room for more believers. Isaiah and the children of Israel needed to hear that from God. When they lived thousands of years ago, the children of Israel thought they were the only ones who had a Savior. And just as some people don't want just anybody joining their club, the children of Israel didn't think their group should be open to outsiders. But God wanted them to know that anyone who believed in Him was welcome.

Today we might think it strange if someone who looked like he or she didn't "belong" joined us for the children's message. It could be someone much older than you, or someone who wore clothes that didn't look like ours. It might be someone who speaks a language we don't understand. It could be someone richer or poorer than most of us. What if it was a homeless person! Would we be ready to welcome that person to God's Club? God might use the same old Bible passage He used with the children of Israel. "I will gather still others to them besides those already gathered." God always has room for more believers.

Someday God will gather all believers beginning with Adam and Eve, continuing through you and me, and your children, your children's children, your children's children's children, and so on. God will take this crowd of millions to heaven where we'll live with Him in perfect happiness.

Sometimes I've wondered if heaven has enough room. Are there enough tickets, or will God run out of space? We find the answer in the old words of Isaiah. God has room for all believers. You see, Jesus bought tickets for us all. And because Jesus paid for our tickets to heaven, God made room for us. Let's thank Him for that.

Prayer. Dear Jesus, thank You for making room for me in God's kingdom. Please help me tell others there is room for them, too. Amen.

Password

PENTECOST 14: Ex. 6:2–8; Rom. 11:33–36; Matt. 16:13–20

Text. I appeared to Abraham, to Isaac and to Jacob as God Almighty, but by My name the LORD I did not make Myself known to them. ... I will take you as My own people, and I will be your God. Then you will know that I am the LORD your God, who brought you out from under the yoke of the Egyptians. *Ex. 6:3, 7*

Teaching aid. A sheet of heavy paper folded in half. Write "Password" on the outside; write "Jesus" on the inside.

Gospel nugget. God revealed Himself through Jesus Christ as the Savior of all people.

Let's begin with a brief prayer. Dear God, thank You for sending Jesus to save sinners. Help us know more about Him as we listen to today's message. Amen.

(*Hold up the paper marked "Password."*) What is a password? (*Encourage responses.*) Passwords allow you to do things that others can't. For example, some computers ask for a password. The computer will not work if you don't type in the special word that tells the computer it's okay to operate. Usually your password is secret. If you tell anyone your password, they may misuse the computer, and that could be serious.

Long ago, God's name was like a password known only to those who loved Him. Whenever they needed help, they knew just what to say. By calling out "God," they could count on help. Today's Old Testament reading tells how God's people used His name as a password.

The children of Israel were slaves in Egypt for more than 400 years. They felt just like the oxen used to pull heavily loaded wagons. (Oxen are large, cow-like animals. They are very strong.) Oxen were yoked—attached to each other and to a wagon. They had no choice but to pull together when their driver commanded. Listen to these Bible verses from Exodus in which God's people are compared to yoked animals. (*Read the text.*)

Have you ever felt lonely or afraid? Have you ever done something wrong and wanted to hide it? Have you ever said mean words to friends or family? Have you ever been angry with someone for no good reason? Have you ever felt like others blame you for whatever goes wrong? If you have felt any of these ways, then you need to know a password. Let me whisper it and show it to you. (*Whisper "Jesus" and open the folded sheet.*)

Our password is so important that I don't think we should keep it secret. Let's tell everyone the new password for God's people. (*Prompt the children to loudly say, "Jesus."*)

Jesus rescued us from the yoke of sin. When you're frightened, lonely, picked on, or wanting to hide what you've done, you are suffering from sin. Sometimes you don't even do anything to feel that way, but that's how sin works. When we feel like that, we simply have to say the password. What was it again? (*Encourage response.*) Yes, "Jesus"! (*Show the password again.*) Jesus takes away our sins and makes us holy. Let's thank Him for that.

Prayer. Dear Jesus, thank You for forgiving me, and thank You for rescuing me when I suffer because of sin. Help me remember Your name, the password that brings joy and peace. Oh yes, Jesus, help me share the password with others, too. Amen.

The Case of the Broken Glass _____

PENTECOST 15: Jer. 15:15–21; Rom. 12:1–8; Matt. 16:21–26

Text. Therefore this is what the LORD says: "If you repent, I will restore you that you may serve Me; if you utter worthy, not worthless, words, you will be My spokesman. Let this people turn to you, but you must not turn to them. I will make you a wall to this people, a fortified wall of bronze; they will fight against you but will not overcome you, for I am with you to rescue and save you," declares the LORD. "I will save you from the hands of the wicked and redeem you from the grasp of the cruel." *Jer. 15:19–21*

Teaching aids. A broken drinking glass placed in a box or other container.

Gospel nugget. God provides sinners opportunities to repent and therefore receive forgiveness for Christ's sake.

This morning you will hear the case of the broken drinking glass. Here lies the victim. (*Reveal the broken glass.*) This broken glass once lived happily in a kitchen cabinet. It gleefully wrapped itself around tangy lemonade, icy cold water, fresh orange juice, silky smooth milk, and bubbly soft drinks. But can it ever refresh thirsty lips again? Of course not. If this glass could speak, it would tell you this sad tale.

I was sitting on the shelf just waiting to be filled. Oh, how I loved to work! But those careless kids ruined it all for me. They played outside all afternoon, tossing the Frisbee until they were sweaty and thirsty. Now, thirst I can handle, but not sweat. All six kids rushed into the kitchen, threw open the cabinet door, and jabbed their sweaty hands into my space on the shelf. I slipped from hand to hand and rolled around on the shelf. Suddenly, I was falling through space. I saw the kitchen floor rushing toward me— well, really I was rushing toward it. Then I heard the terrible crack and the tinkling only broken glass can make. And here I am, shattered and no good, and it's not even my fault.

What a sad story! Have you ever felt like this broken glass? Perhaps you have. Were you ever sick? What was wrong? (*Invite responses.*) We get sick because the world is sick. It's sick with sin! God didn't invent germs and viruses to make us ill. The devil with his evil bag of sins uses germs and viruses to make people miserable. He hopes we become miserable enough to blame God for sickness. But we know better, don't we? When we get sick, we ask Jesus to make us healthy again.

Have you ever felt lonely or like you lost your best friend? Sin separates us from our friends. Sometimes it's their fault and sometimes it's our fault. But when you're feeling sad and lonely, it doesn't matter who is at fault. At times like that we ask Jesus to take away the sins that separate us from others.

One of today's Bible readings tells about a time when God's prophet Jeremiah felt mighty low. He thought his neighbors were against him—and they were! God told Jeremiah not to feel sorry for himself. Listen. (*Read the text.*)

Just as God rescued Jeremiah from sins, He rescues us, too. We can approach God each day and say something like this:

Prayer. Dear God, thank You for sending Jesus to take away my sins. I'm sorry when I do wrong and when I don't do right. I am sad, and I suffer because sin has messed up the world. I know You will make things right for Jesus' sake. Amen.

Watch Out_____

PENTECOST 16: Ezek. 33:7–9; Rom. 13:1–10; Matt. 18:15–20

Text. Son of man, I have made you a watchman for the house of Israel; so hear the word I speak and give them warning from Me. *Ezek. 33:7*

Teaching aid. Anything with a warning label (most over-the-counter medications contain warnings).

Gospel nugget. God tells His people how to live and gives believers the responsibility of sharing that information with others.

(Conduct a brief, exaggerated inspection of the floor or pew before you invite the children to sit.) Before we sit, I want to be sure the area is safe and clean. It looks fine to me, so please sit and we will begin.

Today we will talk about warning signs. I brought one with me. It appears on the label of this medicine, and it says (*read the warning*). The company that makes this medicine wants everyone to know when it is safe and when it is dangerous to use these pills.

You are probably familiar with other warnings and warning signs. Flashing red lights, the sound of bells, and the lowered crossing gates warn that a train is approaching. What might happen if we ignored those warnings and tried to cross the railroad tracks? (*Encourage responses.*) Yes, getting hit by a train would result in death or serious injury.

What must drivers do if they see flashing lights and hear sirens? (*Invite responses.*) Drivers must get out of the way when they see flashing lights and hear sirens. Police cars, ambulances, and fire trucks use flashing lights and wailing sirens to say, "Move over. We're coming through!"

Warning signs and signals are always meant to provide protection. If the warning signs are missing or don't work, people are in danger. If people ignore warning signs or signals, they place themselves in danger.

Does the Bible talk about warnings? Listen to what God says in the book of Ezekiel. (*Read the text.*)

What warnings might a watchman, or security guard, give? (*Invite responses.*) Yes, watchmen usually protect someone's property.

What do God's security guards do? (*Encourage responses.*) God's watchmen warn people about their worst enemies—sin and the devil. In Old Testament days, God sent prophets like Ezekiel to warn His people. He didn't want them to lose faith and become victims of the devil. Do you think people listened to the prophets? Some did. Many didn't. They continued to follow the devil, enjoy their sins, and ignore serious warnings from the prophets. What do you suppose happened when God's people ignored His warnings? (*Invite responses.*) Yes, they threw away their faith and died without believing in God. They will not be in heaven with us.

God makes us watchmen. He wants us to fight against temptations to disobey Him. He wants us to warn others when they are in danger of attack by sin and the devil. And when we or others sin and give in to the devil, we can do another thing—repent. God accepts apologies, and He gives power to overcome temptation.

Let us pray.

Prayer. Dear God, help us watch out for sin and the devil. Make us watchmen to warn others, too. Give us the words and the courage to help others remain faithful. We pray in Jesus' name. Amen.

Happy Ending

PENTECOST 17: Gen. 50:15–21; Rom. 14:5–9;
Matt. 18:21–35

Text. When Joseph's brothers saw that their father was dead, they said, "What if Joseph holds a grudge against us and pays us back for all the wrongs we did to him?" So they sent word to Joseph, saying, "Your father left these instructions before he died: 'This is what you are to say to Joseph: I ask you to forgive your brothers the sins and the wrongs they committed in treating you so badly.' Now please forgive the sins of the servants of the God of your father." When their message came to him, Joseph wept. His brothers then came and threw themselves down before him. "We are your slaves," they said. But Joseph said to them, "Don't be afraid. Am I in the place of God? You intended to harm me, but God intended it for good to accomplish what is now being done, the saving of many lives. So then, don't be afraid. I will provide for you and your children." And he reassured them and spoke kindly to them. *Gen. 50:15–21*

Teaching aids. A slice of bread on a plate.

Gospel nugget. While we are yet sinners, God forgives us for Jesus' sake.

(*Set the bread in front of the children.*) I have one very valuable slice of bread on this plate. How much would you pay for one slice of delicious, filling, nourishing bread, crusts included? (*Encourage responses.*) Now imagine yourself nearly dead because you are starving. You hear that the only bread available is from a person you once treated badly. In fact, you threw him out of his home, hoping he would never return. Would you ask that person for bread?

In one of today's Bible readings we heard about Joseph and his evil brothers. They threw Joseph out of his home and sold him to slave traders. Can you imagine how Joseph felt, treated so terribly by his own family? You would think he was sad, frightened, and angry. But Joseph became the best slave in Egypt. The Egyptians even gave him an important job. God helped Joseph plan for a famine—a time when little food was available because the farm crops failed. Because of Joseph, the people of Egypt had plenty to eat while people in other countries had little.

Joseph's family lived in one of those "other" countries. Joseph gave his brothers the food they needed, and then they felt guilty about how they had mistreated him. Listen to how Joseph's brothers tried to cover up their guilty feelings. (*Read the text.*)

We all like stories with happy endings. That's why the Joseph story is a favorite of many. The Joseph story reminds us of our own story.

We are like Joseph's brothers. But our forgiving brother is Jesus. Our sins caused God to send Jesus away from heaven and place Him on earth so He could suffer and die. How badly we need forgiveness! We know forgiveness comes only through Jesus. Because of our sins He died on the cross. But Jesus invites us to come to Him. He says, "Although I had to die for your sins, I still love you. I forgive you, and I'll always take care of you." And we can return to Jesus every day to hear Him say again, "Of course I forgive you. I've taken away all your sins."

We pray.

Prayer. Dear God, thank You for sending Jesus to give a happy ending to our story. Help us forgive others just as Joseph forgave his family and just as Jesus forgives us. Amen.

How Far Is God?____

PENTECOST 18: Is. 55:6–9; Phil. 1:1–5 (6–11),
19–27; Matt. 20:1–16

Text. Seek the LORD while He may be found; call on Him while He is near. Let the wicked forsake his way and the evil man his thoughts. Let him turn to the LORD, and He will have mercy on him, and to our God, for He will freely pardon. "For My thoughts are not your thoughts, neither are your ways My ways," declares the LORD. "As the heavens are higher than the earth, so are My ways higher than your ways and My thoughts than your thoughts. *Is. 55:6–9*

Teaching aid. Use a pencil to make a small dot on a sheet of plain white paper. Ask an adult to hold up the paper at a distance on your cue.

Gospel nugget. Jesus is near, ready to hear our repentance and forgive us.

Face the back of the church where (*name of assistant*) is holding a piece of paper. What do you see on the paper? I assure you that something is on that page, but we are too far to see it clearly. Perhaps (*assistant*) will bring it closer.

Thank you for your assistance, (*assistant*). Now let's take a closer look at the paper. (*Inspect the paper with the children.*) What do you see? A small dot was on the paper, but we didn't know it. The paper was far away, so the dot seemed invisible.

God seemed like that tiny dot to people living thousands of years ago. He promised a Savior to take away sin so people could be holy like Him. And while people waited for God to keep His promise, He sent prophets to remind them about the coming Savior. The prophets told God's people that He was really nearby though they couldn't see Him. He wanted to forgive their sins even before the Savior was born. Listen to what God told the prophet Isaiah to say. (*Read the text.*)

At just the right time, God sent Jesus to the people. How happy they were! Unlike the promise that always seemed far off, God came to them nearby as a human like themselves. They saw Him heal people, and they listened to His words of love and forgiveness. They watched Jesus die on the cross. Afterwards, His closest friends enjoyed His company. Then one day Jesus left to wait in heaven for all His people. No wonder Jesus sometimes seems far away!

Jesus seems far away when things go wrong. We often do not behave as we should. And if we don't get caught in our bad behavior, we might think Jesus doesn't know about it. After all, He's far away in heaven. Right? Right. And wrong.

Jesus is God and God is everywhere. We can hide nothing from God. And we don't need to hide because He is ready to forgive. We can repent whenever we do wrong—even if no one else catches us. Let's try repenting right now. Pray with me by repeating the words after I say them.

Dear Jesus, ... I'm sorry. ... I'm sorry I don't always obey Mom and Dad. ... I'm sorry I don't always love other people. ... And I'm sorry that I sometimes do things I shouldn't. ... Please forgive me. ... Amen. ...

I have great news for you, kids. Jesus heard us repent, and He forgives us. Since Jesus is nearby, He will help us live and act better. Let's do it!

*Belonging*_____

PENTECOST 19: Ezek. 18:1–4, 25–32; Phil. 2:1–5 (6–11); Matt. 21:28–32

Text. For every living soul belongs to Me, the father as well as the son—both alike belong to Me. The soul who sins is the one who will die. ... Because he considers all the offenses he has committed and turns away from them, he will surely live; he will not die. Yet the house of Israel says, "The way of the Lord is not just." Are My ways unjust, O house of Israel? Is it not your ways that are unjust? *Ezek. 18:4, 28–29*

Teaching aids. The parents or adults who brought the participants to church.

Gospel nugget. God claims us as His own children and offers forgiveness of sins.

Who brought you to church today? (*Encourage responses.*) God blessed you this morning by having someone bring you here. (*Speaking to the congregation.*) If you brought one of these children to church, please stand up. Let's thank God for these people right now. We pray. Heavenly Father, thank You for giving us moms, dads, relatives, and friends to care for us. Thank You for helping them care enough to bring us to worship You. Amen.

You may sit down. (*Speaking to the children.*) Doesn't it feel good to belong to someone? When we belong to someone like moms, dads, relatives, or others who love us, we feel safe and happy. We know that someone is always there when we need them.

How horrible it would be if we didn't belong to someone! That's how the children of Israel felt long, long ago. Oh, they had moms, dads, relatives, and others who cared. But sometimes they didn't belong to God. These children of Israel were quite rude and disrespectful at times. They especially didn't like it when God punished them for doing wrong. "Unfair! Unjust!" they cried. That's when God asked the prophet Ezekiel to speak with the Israelites. Here is what he said. (*Read the text.*) *Unjust* and *unfair* mean about the same thing.

God reminded the children of Israel that they belonged to Him. He had a long history of caring for them and forgiving their many sins. In other words, God loved them. Can someone who loves you also punish you? Of course. In fact, punishment is meant to change poor behavior into better behavior. When the Israelites enjoyed their wrongdoing and loved their sins, God punished them. He invited them to apologize for their sinfulness and to act like they belonged to Him again. Did that make God unfair? Absolutely not!

You belong to those adults who stood up a while ago. Do you also belong to God? Yes, you are God's children. Because we are God's children, He wants us to behave like His children. God knows, however, that our behavior isn't perfect. That's why God did a very unfair thing. He commanded Jesus to live a perfect life for us. Jesus left heaven, and He came to earth where there was sadness and hatred. Is that fair? Of course not. Then God was even more unfair. He told Jesus to suffer and die for our sins! Jesus obeyed. He took the worst punishment for our sins. Why? Jesus wants us to belong to God. He always cares for us, even when He lets us suffer for the wrong we do. That's just God's way of saying, "Hey, wake up. Did you forget that you belong to Me? I don't want to lose you, so I'll help you to remember."

We pray.

Prayer. Dear heavenly Father, thank You for making us Your children. Remind us to be faithful even when it means punishment to help us. Give us the power to live like Your holy children for Jesus' sake. Amen.

Grapes

PENTECOST 20: *Is. 5:1–7; Phil. 3:12–21; Matt. 21:33–43*

Text. He dug it up and cleared it of stones and planted it with the choicest vines. He built a watchtower in it and cut out a wine press as well. Then he looked for a crop of good grapes, but it yielded only bad fruit. *Is. 5:2*

Teaching aids. Gardening tools such as a small rake and shovel.

Gospel nugget. God made us His people and prepared us for service to Him.

I suppose it's a little late in the year to use these. (*Indicate the tools.*) Rakes and shovels are useful in spring when people plant flowers and vegetables. We use rakes to scrape off rocks, twigs, and other junk that clutter up the garden. Shovels help us dig out buried stones and make holes for seeds. The results? We enjoy several months of pretty flowers and fresh vegetables. Unless trouble enters the garden.

What can spoil a garden? (*Encourage responses.*) Good gardens must escape bugs, weeds, too much or too little rain, hungry animals, and the neighborhood kids playing ball. Well-cared-for gardens usually make it past all those dangers. But even well-cared-for gardens sometimes fail because the plants themselves are weak.

The Bible compares God's people to a garden of grapes. Listen to what Isaiah said about God and His people. (*Read the text.*)

Back in Old Testament days, God's people were called Israelites. Sometimes they were called grapes! Now you and I might get angry if someone called us grapes, but grapes were very important back in those days. God's people used grapes to make wine, and wine was important because pure drinking water was sometimes hard to find. As you might imagine, it was an honor to be called grapes back then.

God said that He prepared a fertile field, and He expected a good harvest of plump, juicy grapes. God meant that He chose the Israelites as His people, and He wanted them to love and obey Him. If you listened to the entire Old Testament lesson, you know what happened to God's grape garden. The grapes were bad. They were bad even though they lived in a good garden. God meant that His people did bad things even though He took care of them.

Who are God's people today? We are His new grapes! How does God help us grow? (*Encourage responses.*) God makes sure we have food and places to live. He sends people to love us and whom we love in return. Best of all, God provides faith in Jesus who died to take away our sins. He gives us Christian homes, schools, churches, and Sunday schools to make our faith stronger and healthier.

What are some dangers to your faith? (*Invite responses.*) The devil and our sinful selves are as busy as bugs attacking a garden. They want us to shrivel up and die like the grapes in today's Bible lesson. But we have the Holy Spirit on our side, making us hate sin and love God. And even when we give in to temptation, as we do each day, the Holy Spirit reminds us to say we are sorry and ask God's forgiveness. In fact, the Holy Spirit talks to God for us. Because the Holy Spirit always knows what is good for us, He tells God what we need.

Are all you grapes ready to close with prayer?

Prayer. Dear Lord, thank You for taking care of us. Send Your Holy Spirit to guide us in all we think, say, and do. We pray in our Savior's name. Amen.

1001 Uses

PENTECOST 21: Is. 25:6–9; Phil. 4:4–13; Matt. 22:1–10 (11–14)

Text. On this mountain the LORD Almighty will prepare a feast of rich food for all peoples, a banquet of aged wine—the best of meats and the finest of wines. On this mountain He will destroy the shroud that enfolds all peoples, the sheet that covers all nations; He will swallow up death forever. The Sovereign LORD will wipe away the tears from all faces; He will remove the disgrace of His people from all the earth. The LORD has spoken. In that day they will say, "Surely this is our God; we trusted in Him, and He saved us. This is the LORD, we trusted in Him; let us rejoice and be glad in His salvation." *Is. 25:6–9*

Teaching aid. A roll of paper towels, preferably white.

Gospel nugget. Jesus Christ delivered us from death and meets all our needs.

Paper towels are marvelous. (*Indicate the towels.*) Name some things for which paper towels are good. (*Encourage responses.*)

Paper towels are good mostly for cleaning things. But if we think really hard, I believe we could find some creative uses for paper towels. We could use paper towels for a napkin (*remove a sheet and tuck it into the neck of your shirt*). If we get sloppy while eating, the paper towel will protect our clothes. We could even use it as a tiny table cloth (*demonstrate*) to protect our food from dirt.

Suppose someone was crying. Would paper towels dry their tears? (*Demonstrate.*) And if we wanted to hide something, we could place a paper towel over it. If we wanted to show what was under the cover, we could simply remove the towel, tear it up, and throw it out. (*Demonstrate.*) Paper towels have a 1001 uses.

Paper towels make me think of Jesus, especially after I heard today's Old Testament reading. Listen. (*Read the text.*)

Paper towels remind me of the "shroud that enfolds all peoples, the sheet that covers all nations." God pictured sin as something covered by a shroud or sheet, just as a paper towel can cover something. (*Demonstrate.*) People want to hide their sins from God, but they can't. The only thing they can do is keep themselves from seeing God. The sheet covers their eyes like a blindfold, or shroud. (*Demonstrate.*) But what did God do to the sheet according to Isaiah? He removed it so people could see their Savior. They remembered how much they displeased and angered God with their sins. And the same sheet that once covered their eyes now wiped away their tears. No wonder Isaiah said, "Let us rejoice and be glad in His salvation."

I will give each of you a paper towel. Take it home to remind you how much Jesus loves you. Don't be afraid to use it, either. If you spill something, wipe it up. Let it remind you of how Jesus wipes away our dirty sins and makes us clean again. Besides, you probably have more paper towels at home, just as we have an endless supply of Jesus' love. "Let us rejoice and be glad in His salvation!"

Please pray with me.

Prayer. Lord Jesus, You are even better than paper towels! Dry our tears when we are sad or hurt. Uncover our eyes when we need to see our sinfulness. Wipe away our filthy sins and make us more like You. Let us soak up Your love and share it with others. Amen.

*Limitless*_____

PENTECOST 22: Is. 45:1–7; 1 Thess. 1:1–5a; Matt. 22:15–21

Text. I am the LORD, and there is no other; apart from Me there is no God. I will strengthen you, though you have not acknowledged Me, so that from the rising of the sun to the place of its setting men may know there is none besides Me. I am the LORD, and there is no other. *Is. 45:5–6*

Teaching aids. A cross, Bible, Sunday school lesson leaflet, and a small radio.

Gospel nugget. Our powerful God uses nonbelievers and nonreligious things to accomplish His will.

Look at these items—a cross, a radio, a Bible, and a Sunday school lesson leaflet. Which doesn't belong in the group? (*Invite responses and ask why.*) I think we agree the radio doesn't belong.

(*Hold up the cross.*) The cross is a symbol for Jesus because He died on a cross to take away our sins. We expect to see Christians decorate their church with crosses and to wear crosses as jewelry.

(*Hold up the Bible.*) The Bible tells what God did for people. It tells how God chose the children of Israel as special people, and how He gave them the Promised Land—a place where they could live in peace. In a way, the Bible is a history book. It tells what people did—how they sinned and how they tried to stop God from saving His people. It also tells everything God did to save you and me.

(*Hold up the Sunday school lesson leaflet.*) This Sunday school leaflet contains a lesson from the Bible. It helps us learn more about God's love, and it suggests ways that we can show our love for God.

The three items we have looked at so far are religious things—a cross, a Bible, and a Sunday school lesson leaflet. But the radio is different. (*Hold up the radio.*) It isn't a religious thing. Radios broadcast news, weather, music, and talk shows. We don't expect to see a radio on the altar. (*Point to the altar.*) But can you think of a way radios might help religion? (*Encourage responses.*)

We could search the radio stations for Christian music or messages. Sometimes God uses things that aren't religious, like radios, to broadcast His message. Listen to part of today's religion lesson from the Old Testament. (*Read the text.*)

We know there is only one true God. We know He can do anything with His power—even use radios to spread His Good News. But when God spoke those words thousands of years ago, He was talking to someone who didn't believe in Him. The man's name was Cyrus. Cyrus was to rescue God's people from their enemy, the Babylonians. The Babylonians captured God's people and made them prisoners. Worse yet, they weren't free to worship the true God. In fact, they were in danger of forgetting Him. God's people could not escape or rescue themselves, so God chose an unbeliever to do the job. Without even knowing he was serving God, Cyrus helped free God's people. God helps people however He wants!

You and I need rescue, too. We are sinners with no way to escape or to rescue ourselves. God sent Jesus to do the job. Jesus died on the cross, which sounds like He failed to get the job done. But God brought Jesus back to life and showed His power over sin and death.

We pray.

Prayer. Dear God, thank You for the many ways You love us and share Your Word with us. Bring Your love and Your Word to people everywhere so they may believe in You, too. We pray in Jesus' name. Amen.

Exactly the Same_____

PENTECOST 23: Lev. 19:1–2, 15–18;
1 Thess. 1:5b–10; Matt. 22:34–40 (41–46)

Text. The LORD said to Moses, "Speak to the entire assembly of Israel and say to them: Be holy because I, the LORD your God, am holy. ... Do not pervert justice; do not show partiality to the poor or favoritism to the great, but judge your neighbor fairly. Do not go about spreading slander among your people. Do not do anything that endangers your neighbor's life. I am the LORD. Do not hate your brother in your heart. Rebuke your neighbor frankly so you will not share in his guilt. Do not seek revenge or bear a grudge against one of your people, but love your neighbor as yourself. I am the LORD." *Lev. 19:1–2, 15–18*

Teaching aid. A matching pair of anything, such as socks.

Gospel nugget. By the power of the Holy Spirit, God enables believers to become like Jesus.

Do you know anyone who looks exactly like you? We don't find many people who are exact look-alikes, but we have many examples of exact copies. Take these socks for example—an exact pair. Each looks just like the other. Now look around. What other exact copies do you see? (*Encourage responses. Examples may include pews or chairs, windows, doors, candle sets, etc.*)

Do you know that God wants you to be a copy of Him? He said so in today's reading from the Old Testament. Let's listen again to those words from the book of Leviticus. (*Read the text.*)

There you have it. God said, "Be holy because I, the LORD your God, am holy." God means that we should not sin. He wants us to love Him and love others perfectly. Quite an easy task, wouldn't you say? Not so.

Let's look more closely at the rules God gave His people. First, God said to judge our neighbors fairly. We shouldn't treat rich neighbors better than poor neighbors. But we shouldn't think rich neighbors are bad just because they have lots of money. Are you good at treating all people the same? Do you like sitting next to a kid in school who has old, worn clothes or cheap gym shoes? I think we're all guilty of behavior like that. We're not quite as holy as God expects.

Second, God said to avoid slander. Slander is spreading false information about others. Suppose you get angry with a friend, so you tell other kids not to trust him, that he is a liar and a cheat. Wow! That makes your former friend look bad to others. We're all guilty of slander at times, aren't we?

We don't do much better with God's other rules either. Sometimes we hate others and want to hurt them when they hurt us. And we might refuse to quietly tell others they are doing something wrong or dangerous. Once again, we are far less holy than God expects. But what can we do about it?

First, we can admit our mistakes and our sins. Second, we can remind God about what Jesus did for us. He took our sins away. Third, we can ask for God's help. Let's do that now.

We pray.

Prayer. Lord God, we want to be holy like You. We know we often fail, and we ask Your forgiveness. Thank You for sending Jesus to make us holy. Now send the Holy Spirit to each of us that we may act like Your holy people. Amen.

Right Reasons _____

PENTECOST 24: Amos 5:18–24; 1 Thess. 4:13–14 (15–18); Matt. 23:37–39 or Matt. 25:1–13

Text. But let justice roll on like a river, righteousness like a never-failing stream! *Amos 5:24*

Teaching aid. A puppet (see Lent 5).

Gospel nugget. Our good works are acceptable through Jesus Christ.

Presenter: Good morning, boys and girls. My puppet (*indicate the puppet*) wanted to do a good work today so he volunteered to help with the children's message.

Puppet: Hi, boys and girls. Today's special Bible message comes from the book of Amos. (*Read the text.*) Oh, I love that Bible passage, I do!

Presenter: It is an excellent passage, but why do you like it?

Puppet: 'Cause I'm ready for God to send Jesus back to earth. Then He will roll out His justice on all the evil sinners of the world.

Presenter: That sounds frightening.

Puppet: Yep. But I'm ready.

Presenter: I'm sure you are, now we should …

Puppet (*interrupting*): Ahem! Don't you and the kids want to know why I'm ready?

Presenter: I think we know, now …

Puppet (*interrupting*): No, you don't know! I will tell you why I'm ready for God to send Jesus on Judgment Day. You see, I've worked very hard at being good. I take out the garbage, dry the dishes, feed the cat, clean the canary cage (not at the same time, of course) …

Presenter (*interrupting*): Wait a minute. You get paid an allowance for those jobs, don't you?

Puppet: Yes, but what difference does that make?

Presenter: Would you do those jobs if you didn't get paid?

Puppet: Welllll, I need money. I'd probably seek employment elsewhere. But you didn't let me finish. I remind you that I come to church and Sunday school every Sunday. And (*importantly*) I am helping you right now, aren't I?

Presenter: Yes, you're helping. But I don't think you will like what I have to say.

Puppet (*indignant*): Here I am, Mr. Good Guy, and what do I get? I get treated like a dirty old sock (*glove*). I could have just stayed on someone's foot (*hand*), you know!

Presenter: That's right. If you think so highly of your wonderful deeds, perhaps you should do something else. You quoted your favorite verse from Amos before, but did you listen to the rest of the Amos passage this morning?

Puppet: I didn't like that part, so I forgot it.

Presenter: Amos told how angry God was with His people. They were doing good things but for wrong reasons. I guess they wanted to show God how good they were—you know, impress Him so He would take them to heaven.

Puppet: Sounds good to me.

Presenter: Oh no. We don't get to heaven by impressing God with our goodness. Jesus impressed God by living a perfect life in place of the imperfect lives we live. Jesus did everything right because He obeyed God and gave Him glory. He did the right things for the right reasons. Then Jesus died to take away our sins and make us holy in God's sight. Now that Jesus did His good work, God accepts our good works.

Puppet (*sheepishly*): I think it's time for prayer. May I?

Presenter: Go ahead.

Puppet: Dear God, I want to do good things in Your name. I know You will like what I do because Jesus makes me and what I do holy in Your sight. Help me obey You and do what You want— for the right reasons. Amen.

Led by Love_____

PENTECOST 25: Hos. 11:1–4, 8–9; 1 Thess. 5:1–11; Matt. 24:3–14 or Matt. 25:14–30

Text. I led them with cords of human kindness, with ties of love; I lifted the yoke from their neck and bent down to feed them. … I will not carry out My fierce anger, nor will I turn and devastate Ephraim. For I am God, and not man—the Holy One among you. I will not come in wrath. *Hos. 11:4, 9*

Teaching aids. A short length of clothesline or a strip of cloth; arrange in advance for a volunteer who is willing to have his or her hands tied.

Gospel nugget. God shows us mercy for Christ's sake instead of giving us what we deserve.

What do you think the police used to keep criminals from getting away before handcuffs were invented? (*Invite responses.*) Law officers probably tied the criminals' hands with ropes. They probably did it like this. (*Demonstrate. Tie the volunteer's hands gently behind his or her body. Leave a length of rope or cloth as a "leader."*)

A criminal tied like this couldn't use his hands, and he could be led to jail by pulling on the leader. As you might imagine, anyone could treat prisoners roughly by yanking on the rope or leading them where walking was difficult. If anyone complained about the rough treatment, the police officer could say, "He broke the law. He deserves this treatment."

None of us want to be tied up and led like criminals. In some ways, however, we are criminals who break the law regularly. Whose laws do we break? (*Invite responses.*) Everyone here is guilty of breaking God's laws.

Back in Old Testament days, God made 10 laws to obey. They were good laws, too. Had people obeyed, life would have been happy. God would have been happy, too. Sadly, no one could obey those laws. There was just too much sin in the world. All God's people deserved to be tied up like criminals (*indicate the tied volunteer*), and led to their punishment. But that wasn't God's way.

God sent Jesus to remove the ropes from sinners. Listen again to a portion of this morning's reading from the book of Hosea. (*Read the text.*)

God leads people with ropes called "cords of human kindness" and "ties of love." Those don't sound like rough ropes to me. (*Remove the rope from the volunteer.*) Does this mean God's people no longer break His laws? No, we still disobey His laws even though Jesus reduced the number from ten to two. The two laws Jesus wants us to obey are laws of love—love God and love other people. But we don't always obey these laws either. So Jesus obeyed them for us.

Jesus obeyed God the Father, and you know what happened. He took our sins away and promised us a place in heaven. And while we're on earth, God sends the Holy Spirit to lead us with cords of kindness and ties of love. The Holy Spirit guides us to church and Sunday school. We want to love others and love God because the Holy Spirit leads us to love them. Let's thank God for leading us.

Prayer. Dear God, thank You for leading us—first, to faith in You and second, to serve others with the same kind of love You show us. We pray in Jesus' name. Amen

*Taking Out the Trash*_____

Text. Man born of woman is of few days and full of trouble. He springs up like a flower and withers away; like a fleeting shadow, he does not endure. Do you fix your eye on such a one? Will you bring him before you for judgment? Who can bring what is pure from the impure? No one! Man's days are determined; you have decreed the number of his months and have set limits he cannot exceed. So look away from him and let him alone, till he has put in his time like a hired man. *Job 14:1–6*

Teaching aid. A garbage bag.

Gospel nugget. God trashes our sins for Jesus' sake.

Do you ever feel like giving up? Okay, then you know how I felt about this children's message! My job is to explain today's Old Testament reading, but did you hear it? Ugh! I'm a good-news person, and today's reading from Job sounds horrible. I wanted to cut those words out of the Bible, seal them in this bag (*indicate the trash bag*), and toss them into the garbage! Listen as I read those six sad verses again. (*Read the text.*)

Job complained that people are like flowers—they grow and then they wither away. Job claimed that people didn't have a chance to be what God wants them to be—they don't live long enough! Then he told God to just leave us alone. There was nothing we sinners could do to make life better. Do you agree with Job?

Job was wrong when he told God to leave him alone. God uses suffering to bring us closer to Him. And Job was also wrong about giving up and giving in to sin. Fortunately, Job realized how wrong he was. Listen to what he said shortly after he complained to God.

"If a man dies, will he live again? All the days of my hard service I will wait for my renewal to come. You will call and I will answer You; You will long for the creature Your hands have made. Surely then You will count my steps but not keep track of my sin. My offenses will be sealed up in a bag; You will cover over my sin" (Job 14:14–17).

Wow! Now that's a message I enjoy sharing. And you know what? That good news sounds extra good because the bad news sounded extra bad! Hey, do you suppose God planned it that way?

It's no secret that we can't be good enough to earn God's love or a place in heaven. If those were the only things we knew, I believe we might be right in giving up and giving in to sin. Our life would be trash! (*Indicate the bag.*)

Thank God our life isn't trash. In fact, our sins are trash, and the holy trash man took the garbage away. Who is that holy trash man? Yes, it was Jesus. When Jesus suffered and died to take away our sins, it was like He placed every sin in a huge trash bag (*indicate the bag again*) and burned it in a hot fire. Now when God sees us, it's just as Job said. Surely, God does not keep track of our sins because Jesus takes out the trash every day.

Please pray with me.

Prayer. Lord Jesus, thank You for trashing our sins. Please strengthen us, and help us become more like You. Amen.

All Gone _____

SECOND-LAST SUNDAY IN THE CHURCH YEAR:
Jer. 25:30–32 or Jer. 26:1–6; 1 Thess. 1:3–10 or
1 Thess. 3:7–13; Matt. 25:31–46 or Matt. 24:1–14

Text. "The tumult will resound to the ends of the earth, for the LORD will bring charges against the nations; He will bring judgment on all mankind and put the wicked to the sword," declares the LORD. *Jer. 25:31*

Teaching aids. Jer. 26:13 written out in pencil on one side of a sheet of paper; *sin* written on the opposite side; an eraser.

Gospel nugget. Jesus will eradicate sin when He comes in judgment.

From which Old Testament book did the pastor read today? He used the book of Jeremiah. Have you heard of him? Jeremiah was a famous prophet, although he might have preferred less fame. God's people, the Israelites, never proclaimed a "Jeremiah Day" to honor him, nor did they show him much respect even though God Himself spoke to Jeremiah. In fact, the Israelites hated Jeremiah. More than once, they wanted to kill him.

The people hated Jeremiah because they hated God. And why did they hate God? They hated God because He wanted people to obey Him and to worship Him alone. God used Jeremiah to say this: (*Read and show the text.*)

God's people didn't like hearing what would happen if they failed to correct their bad behavior. They figured they would be happier if God's messenger was gone. They also thought they would be happier if God was gone. Instead of allowing the Israelites to hate Him and suffer later for their sin, God warned them what would happen if they didn't change. And God also gave them many opportunities to change. See what Jeremiah said. (*Indicate the paper.*) "Now reform your ways and your actions and obey the LORD your God. Then the LORD will relent and not bring the disaster He has pronounced against you" (Jer. 26:13). But here is what those ungrateful people did. (*Erase the text from the paper.*)

They got rid of God's Word. They nearly got rid of Jeremiah. And for awhile, God left, and they were alone. People cannot live without God.

Many years later, God sent Jesus to teach and show His love. Some people loved Jesus and listened. They believed and were saved. Others wanted to erase (*hold up the eraser*) Jesus. They hated Him because He called them sinners. They hated Jesus because He told them to change their evil ways or they would be punished. Instead of thanking Jesus for the wonderful warning, they killed Him. And even when Jesus rose from the dead, they still didn't believe He was their Savior.

As God promised back in the days of Jeremiah, and as He promised again when Jesus rose into heaven, Jesus will return with His own eraser someday. What will Jesus do with His eraser? (*Indicate the eraser.*) Yes, He will erase sin forever. (*Demonstrate.*) Sin will disappear. That's great news for all of us here because we believe in Jesus. He erased our sins, and we need not fear the day when Jesus comes again. But those who refuse to believe in Jesus have much to fear. Let's pray for them.

Prayer. Dear Jesus, thank You for making us faithful Christians. Help others accept God's words of warning. Then invite them to You for forgiveness. We want all people to celebrate in heaven when sin is all gone. Amen.

Answers and Questions_____

LAST SUNDAY IN THE CHURCH YEAR:
Is. 65:17–25; 2 Peter 3:3–4, 8–10a, 13 or
1 Cor. 15:20–28; Matt. 25:1–13 or Matt. 25:31–46

Text. Before they call I will answer; while they are still speaking I will hear. *Is. 65:24*

Teaching aids. A telephone and a Bible; a current newspaper.

Gospel nugget. Jesus promises to take believers to His new kingdom of unimaginable joy.

This morning I plan to discuss several problems with you, so I brought along a telephone in case we want to ask God's advice. We'll call Him if we need His help.

Have you noticed how easily things fall apart? Perhaps it's a toy that breaks soon after you buy it or one that doesn't work at all, even when brand new. More seriously, it seems that pollution, earthquakes, and storms wreck what we expect to last. I think I'll call God and ask Him about this problem. (*Pick up the receiver, but don't dial. Simulate a phone conversation.*) Oh, hello. Someone is already on this line. Oh! It's God with an answer even before I asked Him the question. That's God though. He's always a few steps ahead of us. What's that, God? You know how things get ruined on earth? I see. Okay, we'll wait for Your word. (*Hang up.*) God says He plans to fix the earth. He'll tell us more later.

Problem one was easy. Now on to problem two—death. Would you agree that death is a problem? Death usually saddens